MARK BRANDON READ

CHOPPER 9

MARK BRANDON READ

CHOPPER 9

SOME DON'T LIKE IT HOT

JOHN BLAKE

Published by John Blake Publishing Ltd,
3 Bramber Court, 2 Bramber Road,
London W14 9PB, England

www.johnblakepublishing.co.uk

First published in paperback in 2009

ISBN: 978 1 84454 800 2

British Library Cataloguing-in-Publication Data:

A catalogue record for this book is available from the British Library.

Design by www.envydesign.co.uk

Printed in Great Britain by CPI Bookmarque, Croydon, CR0 4TD

1 3 5 7 9 10 8 6 4 2

©

Papers used by John Blake Publishing are natural, recyclable products made
from wood grown in sustainable forests. The manufacturing processes conform
to the environmental regulations of the country of origin.

Every attempt has been made to contact the relevant copyright-holders,
but some were unobtainable. We would be grateful if the appropriate people
could contact us.

CONTENTS

CHAPTER 1

TURKEY HUNT

Gangsters come and gangsters go but lawyers last forever.
MARK BRANDON READ

Aussie Joe Gravano and Salvatore 'Fat Sally' Gigante sat at a private booth in New York's famed Patsy's Restaurant in New York's even more famous West 56th Street.

'Hey, baby, ya ever been turkey hunting?'

The bored waitress looked down at Aussie Joe Gravano. Her face said she'd heard this stupid joke a thousand times from a thousand wiseguys, but Joe kept right on.

'You gobble, I'll shoot. Ha ha ha.'

Joe roared laughing at his own comedy. The waitress worked up a passable imitation of a smile. She survived on tips and that meant smiling at idiots. She turned and walked away while Aussie Joe, still laughing, watched her hips swing in a

2

way that suggested she was a waitress in waiting. Waiting to become either a stripper, a whore or a porn queen.

'Jesus, Joe,' said Sally, 'that fucking joke is old enough to be on the pension.'

'Your trouble is you got no sense of humour,' snarled Joe.

Before the conversation could progress, a third man joined them at the booth.

'How's it going, Carmine?' said Fat Sally, shaking hands with the smooth-looking, well-dressed gent.

Carmine Adonis was a big-money mob lawyer, with a law degree from correspondence school and a Giorgio Armani suit. He sat down and looked at Aussie Joe, waiting for good manners to kick in. Joe ignored him until Fat Sally introduced him to the smiling, evil-looking thug on the other side of the table.

'I'm sorry,' said Sally after a pause. 'Carmine Adonis, meet my cousin all the way from down under, Joey Gravano. We call him Aussie Joe.'

The two men shook hands.

'Australia,' said Adonis. 'I was there recently for the grand opening of the new casino in Melbourne. The Crown ... most impressive.'

Aussie Joe smiled, but knew this smooth lawyer was lying. Joe had been to Las Vegas, and he knew the Crown Casino could probably get a licence as a well-decorated toilet compared with some of the real estate in Vegas. He didn't like being patronised by Americans, even if they were fellow Sicilians.

Unbeknown to his cousin Sally and the slippery silk-suit lawyer, Aussie Joe was in New York for a reason, as well as an all-expenses-paid holiday. He thought he best deal with the reason in extra-quick time, then attend to the holiday.

So he got into character, and smiled at Carmine Adonis the way a pit-bull greets a postman. 'Didn't they use to call you Noodles?' he asked.

Adonis went pale and choked.

Fat Sally laughed. 'Hey, I didn't know that, Carmine.'

'Yeah,' said Joe. 'After Noodles Romanoff.'

Sally looked puzzled.

'Shit,' said Joe patiently. 'Noodles fucking Romanoff – you know, the Roger Ramjet cartoon, you know Roger Ramjet. He's our man, hero of our nation for his adventures, just be sure to stay tuned to this station.'

Carmine Adonis tried to move out of his seat, but Aussie Joe reached out a powerful left hand and took hold of the lawyer's right forearm.

'Don't go, Noodles.'

The lawyer stayed. He was very quiet and very frightened.

'What's this Noodles shit, Carmine? I don't get it,' Fat Sally asked, wondering why the friendly mood of a moment before had turned deadly serious.

'Let me explain, Sally,' said Joe. 'When Carmine here was in the FBI, his nickname was Noodles.'

'What?' whispered Sally. 'But I've know this guy for fuckin' years. Jesus, Joe, you don't even come from here; how do you know anything about anything?'

'Yeah,' said Carmine, breaking his silence to try a bluff, sensing he could have Sally on side.

But Aussie Joe kept the vice-like grip with one hand and reached for his Colt .45 automatic with the other. He carried it down the front of his pants in a concealed clip holster unseen by either of the others. 'You're right,' said Joe. 'I don't know fucking nothing.'

'Yeah, that's right,' said Adonis, appealing to Sally. 'What would this guy know?'

'Shut up,' snarled Sally.

The lawyer was one thing, but Aussie Joe was family. Sally was starting to think. Joe could see the wheels turning in his mind, and helped the process along a little.

'Yeah, Sal, who do ya reckon paid for my ticket over here?' he said softly.

'Jesus Christ,' whispered Sally. 'Pisciotta. Holy hell, Gotti's underboss.'

'Gotti's in prison,' Carmine pleaded. 'He's paranoid out of his head; he thinks everyone's a rat.'

The lawyer didn't see Aussie Joe's right hand come up from under the table, but the waitress did. She was pouring coffee into the cup of a little Jewish man who would always tip her 20 bucks, providing the buttons on her uniform were undone enough for him to get a good eyeful of her rather generous tits and to slip the folded note into her ample cleavage. She screamed as Aussie Joe stuck the barrel of his .45 into Adonis's open mouth and pulled the trigger three times, sending the back of the lawyer's head smashing into the wooden panelling behind him. The bullets splintered the wood as they came out the back of the skull. There wasn't a lot of blood at first. The slugs went in the size of a dime and came out the size of a quarter, and the blood didn't really start until the body fell sideways.

Aussie Joe moved out of his seat. Fat Sally, in a state of shock, slid around the booth and then left the table the same side as his cousin, not really wanting to climb over Adonis's twitching corpse.

As Aussie Joe walked out, he turned to the waitress, who by then had stopped screaming. 'Like I said, honey, you gobble, I'll shoot,' he said, and laughed as he walked out.

Adonis slumped to the floor and the blood leaked out. There was no Quentin Tarantino shower of blood and bone, no rainbow spray flying across the room to cover the poor waitress and her white uniform with red spots. Shoot a bottle of warm beer and you'll get that movie-type shower of liquid spray, but not a human head. In real life you can take a man's head off with a sawn-off shotgun at two feet or two inches and not even get a blood spot on the barrel. Let's just say I know that for a fact. I learned first-hand with the late Sammy the Turk down at Bojangles in St Kilda. The reason being that slugs coming out of the barrel of a gun travel at least at the speed of sound, faster unless it's subsonic ammo, and the slug will go in and come out before the blood flow even has time to notice the new hole that's been made for it.

People who make these bang-bang gangster movies ain't never shot no one, that's easy to see. That scene in *Pulp Fiction* where Vega shoots Marvin in the back of the car, and the whole car, including Travolta and the driver, is covered in blood … well, I'm sorry to say, it's bullshit.

You'd think Tarantino might stop to ask somebody about bullets and blood sprays and such. If blood sprayed forwards every hitman in the world would need a raincoat as well as a gun.

But I digress. There's a story to be told, and I'm telling it.

'Hey, Joe,' said Sally as they walked down the street.

'Yeah, what?' grunted Joe.

'Ya wanna do me a big fucking favour?'

'What?'

'Well,' said Sally, 'next time you shoot someone like that, how about giving me some sort of warning.'

'How do ya mean?' asked Joe.

'Well,' said Sally, 'how about some sort of signal?'

'A signal?' said Joe. 'What? Like a nod or a wink?'

'Yeah,' said Fat Sally. 'Give me a wink.'

Aussie Joe thinks this is quite funny. 'So let me get this right, Sal. Next time I shoot someone you want me to wink at you first?'

'Yeah,' said Sally, seeing nothing funny in it at all. 'Give us a wink first. OK?'

Joe made like a slow learner. 'I promise next time I shoot someone in your company I'll give you a wink,' he said solemnly.

'Thank you,' said Sally with an air of injured dignity. 'I don't think that's too much to ask, Joe. Jesus, ya nearly gave me a heart attack back there.'

Joe hailed a cab. 'OK, OK,' he said. 'Shut up and I promise I'll wink at ya.'

Melbourne, 1977. Young Joey Gravano sat in the lounge of old Pop Kelly's flat in Rockley Road, South Yarra. Their weekly chess game had become a great challenge for the young Sicilian kid. In two years he had never beaten the old gentleman.

As the old man studied the chessboard, Joey tried to distract him with conversation and questions. 'So what happened then, Mr Kelly?' he asked intently.

Old Keith Kelly didn't move his eyes from the chessboard as he spoke. 'Well, Joey, I joined up aged 16 in 1939. The 16th Battalion, Cameron Highlanders. They made me the battalion bugler, then the bloody brigade bugler. Got injured a little bit and sent back to the 118th General Hospital. I turned 21 years old at Toll Plantation.' As Keith Kelly spoke, he removed young Gravano's queen and then said, 'Check.'

Young Joey quickly moved his king, then led him on. 'Yeah, then what, Mr Kelly? What about the Japs?'

'Oh, well,' said Pop Kelly. 'There was a bit of fuss on Moratai in Dutch New Guinea. Like I said, Jackeno Bay, Toll Plantation.'

'No, no,' said young Joey. 'The court martial.'

'Oh,' sighed Pop Kelly as he removed one of Joey's knights and said, 'Check,' again. Joey hurriedly moved his king again.

The old man kept talking. 'That was in 1945, on a Jap casualty clearing station. It went all the way up to 11th Division HQ Major General "Red Robby" Robinson...'

He paused. 'There was this Jap major who spoke perfect

English and he asked me if his men and he could go swimming, so I got permission and off we went. The problem was, I returned without the bastards.'

'How many?' asked Joey.

'Twenty-one in all,' said Pop Kelly, removing another castle from the board and saying, 'Check,' again.

Joey quickly moved his king. 'Then what?' he asked innocently.

'Ah, some Pommy Red Cross officer asked me where the Japs were that I'd taken swimming. I said they swam away. He laughed and said they would be back when they were hungry. Ha, ha.'

'Why did they swim away, Mr Kelly? Did they escape, or what?'

'Nah,' said Pop Kelly. 'I wasn't too keen on the Japs, son, so I machine gunned the bastards in the surf. Ha, ha, ha. I'd killed Jap POWs before. Shit, we all did. Why feed them? Cheaper to shoot 'em.' He laughed again. 'Shit, I'd taken so many Japs swimming and returned without 'em they used to call me the swimming instructor.'

'So how come they tried to court martial you this time, Mr Kelly?' asked Joey.

'Well,' smiled old Keith, 'it might have been because the bloody war had been over for three weeks.'

'So what happened?' asked young Joey, amazed.

'It's like this, son,' said the old man. 'War crimes are never committed by the winners of any war, only the losers. Red Robby had the whinging Pommy Red Cross bloke transferred

9

to shit creek and promptly lost the paperwork. And, as a reward, I got sent on the Cook's tour of Japan with the 34th Brigade on a Yank ship called the Taos Victory with eleven hundred other men, all part of the BCOF Jap holiday unit.

'We landed in Kure on 16 January 1946. I spoke Japanese so I went into signals as an exchange operator, then I got picked to do the SDS run to Tokyo. Even met MacArthur several times.'

Joey made one more move, then heard Mr Kelly say the fatal words as he counter-moved. 'Checkmate.'

Joey sat back and thought to himself, The bloody swimming instructor. Some of these old diggers have seen more cold-blooded murder than all the gangsters in all the world ever see.

He turned to the old man and kept up the conversation. 'Any trouble in Japan, Mr Kelly?'

'Only after curfew, son,' said Pop with a smile. 'Only after curfew. Ha ha.'

Joey looked down at the chessboard and changed the subject.

'The more I attack, the more you win, Mr Kelly. How come? What sort of tactic is that you keep pulling on me?'

'Well, Joey, your own people invented it.'

'My people?' said Joey, his jaw dropping. 'How's that?'

'Yeah,' said Pop. 'It's the art of defence; the art of winning in the face of attack. There are various variations of the tactic, but basically it's the art of defence by using the other fellow's attack against himself.'

'What's it called, Mr Kelly?'

'The Sicilian Defence, son. It's called the Sicilian Defence.'

CHAPTER 2

WHEN IN ROME

Melbourne, 1987. Joey Gravano sat quietly in his first-class seat on a Qantas flight leaving Tullamarine for Rome. He was on his way to visit his Uncle Hector in Palermo, Sicily. Hector Aspanu was a nephew to the long-dead bandit and Sicilian legend Salvatore Juiliano, and that made Joey's uncle part of Sicilian mafia royalty.

Joey had his head stuck in an old book Pop Kelly had given him and was unaware of the Chinese lady next to him. She was a voluptuous young lady who was also slightly annoyed. This was because of Joey's interest in his old book and not in her legs, despite the fact she was crossing and uncrossing them like Sharon Stone on heat.

'What's that you're reading?' she asked at last, determined not to be ignored by a gorilla in a good suit. She had an American accent.

'Book on chess,' said Joey shortly, not even bothering to look up.

'I play chess,' she purred.

'Ya don't say,' said Joey. He wasn't the smoothest bastard you've ever seen, but she kept trying.

'Who wrote it?' she asked.

Joey looked up, slightly annoyed. It was then he realised just what it was sitting next to him.

'Doctor Emanuel Lasker,' he replied. 'World chess champ for 27 years straight. The greatest chess master in history according to many. The man was a strategic and tactical genius, the master of the Sicilian Defence.'

The Chinese lady purred a whisper 'I've never been beaten in chess. French, Dutch, Sicilian Defence, English manoeuvre, Russian attack … I know them all.'

Joey smiled.

'You don't believe me?' the woman asked.

'I didn't say that,' said Joey.

The Chinese lady called the air hostess. It was night-time. The first-class area was in a state of semi-darkness. The hostie was a gorgeous-looking blonde who'd slipped into a bit of the first-class champagne in the galley, by the look of her. The Chinese lady asked about a chessboard and the tipsy air hostess vanished for a few moments before reappearing with a nifty wooden case that opened up into a chessboard.

The Chinese lady set up the board and turned to Joey. 'My name is Simone, by the way. Simone Tao. I work for the Royal

Hong Kong Trading Company, Merchant Banking Division, so you can stop smiling at me like I'm some fool,' she said.

'I'm Joey Gravano. I work for my uncle, Hector Aspanu, of Aspanu International.'

Her eyes flickered slightly as the name registered. Aspanu International was international all right: a global washing machine for mafia drug money, a lot of which passed through Hong Kong banks. She suddenly decided to let this evil-looking Italian beat her at chess. There was such a thing as a tactical retreat, and she knew all about it.

'That's a lovely Rolex watch you have,' she remarked.

'I'll tell you what,' grunted Joey. 'You beat me at chess, it's yours.' He wasn't big on the small talk, Joey, but she understood his type.

'And if you beat me?' she murmured sweetly.

Joey was never a great romantic. He grabbed his swelling crotch with his right hand.

'You get a good go at this,' he said.

Simone smiled. She'd sucked her way up the corporate ladder and if doing the job with this Sicilian hillbilly could get her close to the Aspanu Group it would be a business contact worth its weight in gold.

Eight hours later, Simone Tao got off the plane highly frustrated. She'd beaten him 16 games in a row despite desperately trying to lose. God, thought Simone, he has to be the dumbest Sicilian in the whole world. But she did have his business card. Not to mention the Rolex.

Joey Gravano quietly walked out of Leonardo Da Vinci Airport at Fiumicino, near Rome. He travelled light and carried no luggage. Even if he had any it wouldn't have mattered, because the mob controlled the whole airport and Customs was never a problem – except for long-legged Chinese ladies. Italians being Italians, the Customs officers took one look at the lovely Simone Tao and promptly took her to a private room for a full strip search. Joey smiled at this. He knew the inspectors. If she tried to protest against a full cavity search, she would spend her holiday in a holding facility until she agreed. Still smiling at this comical thought, he hailed a taxi and had himself taken to the Hotel Hassler Villa Medici in Rome. The best hotel in the city for a long sleep.

Sure enough, Simone Tao suffered the indignity of having a large fat Customs inspector's hand poking around her most private parts.

She walked out of Fiumicino Airport like a rape victim. She wondered if her Sicilian chess partner had anything to do with her recent embarrassment as she had noticed the same inspector wave him through like visiting royalty.

As she got into a taxi she decided to think herself lucky. A Chinese girl in Italy, she was lucky it was only a fat hand up her pussy. Who could she protest to? It took 20 or 30 days to post a letter out of Italy, and a complaint would be acted on within about 20 or 30 months. Or not at all.

The taxi ride from the airport to Rome took 45 minutes with the mad cab driver heading in every direction but

Rome while looking into his rear-vision mirror at her legs. She had rooms booked at the Cavalieri Hilton and she couldn't get there quick enough. She knew American money had a magical effect on cab drivers right through Europe, and the 50-dollar bill she handed the driver brought his attention back to the road and away from her legs. After a few minutes of breakneck speeds, she found herself in front of the Cavalieri Hilton.

God, she hated Italy. Great country, but the people were all quite perfectly insane – and they smelled. Didn't anyone take a bath in this country? she thought to herself as she entered the grand doorway of the hotel with her insane taxi driver and several hotel porters in heated argument over who was going to carry her two suitcases. She turned to view this comic sight. God, she thought, I've been fisted at the airport and so far it's been all downhill from there. No wonder they lost the Roman Empire.

Gravano, on the other hand, arrived at his hotel in extra-quick time, and had to force money on a cab driver unwilling to take it. He was then ushered like some Hollywood movie star to the best apartments the hotel had. He bathed, and was in bed sleeping like a baby – a big, ugly baby, admittedly – while on the other side of town a fight had broken out and knives were being pulled over who would carry the bags of the lovely Chinese lady.

When in Rome do as the Chinese do, thought Simone. Bugger the bags, get me to my room.

She never left home without her American Express gold

card. She'd found that money was the only luggage worth carrying. She, too, eventually got to her apartment, bathed and slept.

Tomorrow night, she thought as she drifted off, it will be dinner with Bruno Dietrich at the Cafe Rosati in the Piazza del Popolo. Why all Swiss bankers preferred to conduct business in this shithole of a city was a puzzle to Simone, but there it was.

When flying from Rome to Palermo in Sicily, wise men charter a flight from the military airport of Clampino on the edge of Rome. Joey Gravano was wise enough to do exactly this, and, upon landing at a small airport that was listed on the map only by an Italian military number, Joey then spent a goodly 15 minutes meeting with his uncle Hector in the airport's public toilet.

Uncle Hector watched a hell of a lot of Italian spy movies and loved secret meetings. He was famous for ordering men to travel halfway around the world for a ten-minute meeting at a train station in the middle of nowhere. He tended to overplay the role of the humble peasant Sicilian godfather, and would often meet people wearing dirty, old, torn clothing and a three-day growth of stubble on his face.

Being naturally shy of the tub, he bathed ever so slightly and lived in two rooms above a barber's shop in Palermo's red-light area. His ever-ready bodyguards waited outside the toilet door. Their names were Benny and Bobby Benozzo. The whole sight was a comedy of contradiction as the

Benozzo brothers dressed like Hollywood movie stars and any stranger couldn't help but notice the two expensively dressed thugs walking each side of an old man who looked like the village rat-catcher.

But that was the mafia in Sicily. They fitted in with all the subtlety of a camouflaged neon sign. People just pretended not to notice the fact that an Italian army captain escorted old Don Aspanu and his two well-dressed bodyguards to the toilet to meet Joey. It was hardly covert operational procedure, but that didn't matter in those parts. Nothing mattered except keeping sweet with the mob.

Hector Aspanu handed Joey a photo and began to speak. 'His name is Dietrich, Bruno Dietrich. He's in Rome now. Swiss banker and a Jewish thief. Dietrich is his father's name. His mother's name was Goldbloom. He's staying at the Lord Byron Hotel, has lunch every day at Cafe Rosati. You know, in Piazza del Popolo. All the faggots, writers and artists and the would-be actors get their bloody espresso and shit food there. But he likes to visit the church every day, you know.'

Joey looked puzzled.

Uncle Hector snapped, 'Santa Maria del Popolo. It's the church the fucking square was named after. Ya can't miss it. Jesus Christ, do ya want me to draw ya a fucking map?'

Joey shook his head. 'No, no, Uncle. I got it, I got it. Cafe Rosati.'

Hector kept going. 'You can spot him at the cafe sidewalk tables easy as shit, but I want this thief shot in the church. It's nice and quiet in there and people should die in church, don't ya think?' he said. He wasn't really asking advice. He never did.

Joey nodded diplomatically. 'Yeah, church seems a nice place to die.'

Uncle Hector laughed. 'Even for a make-believe Swiss, pretend German Jew, church is a good place to die. So you do this tomorrow, OK, Joey? Not the day after, but tomorrow.'

'OK. Yeah, sure, Uncle Hector.'

The old man kissed his nephew. 'You a good boy, Joey.'

As character readings go, this was giving Joey a bit the best of it, but family is family, after all. It's not every young man who's willing to shoot people for his uncle.

The Cafe Rosati is on the Piazza del Popolo, a vast airy square or the world's most beautiful car park – take your pick. In one corner was the church, Santa Maria del Popolo. Joey sat at a sidewalk table and waited. His uncle was right – good espresso, shit food. They catered to the American tourist trade, and what would Yanks know about good cooking? Joey went to check his watch, and remembered the Chinese chess player on the plane. Just then, he heard a voice.

'Lost your watch, honey?'

Joey looked up to see the Chinese girl he was day-dreaming about. She was in full summertime glory, almost wearing a tight-cut pair of short white shorts, and her bare honey-coloured legs went all the way down to little white slip-on Italian shoes. Very cute. She wore a white loose-fitting cheesecloth shirt. The splash of solid gold jewellery around her neck and wrists set it all off perfectly, but Joey did feel a certain concern that the shorts might not be quite up to the job of holding her arse in. Even passing priests were doing a double take.

A beautiful Chinese female face has lips that swell in a pouting and a sexy manner under those sexy eyes. It's a teeny bit politically incorrect, but Chinese girls are either dog ugly or ball-breakingly beautiful. Simone Tao was in the second category.

Two Italian actresses – probably porno queens, by the look of them – were sitting at a nearby table. They started slandering the Chinese beauty to each other loudly in Italian. Joey turned and in Italian told the two men they were sitting with, in his unmistakable Collingwood Sicilian accent, that if they didn't shut their whores up he would shoot both men on the spot. A threat like that can be either ignored or taken seriously. The stone-cold silence indicated Joey had been taken seriously.

Simone Tao produced a pair of sunglasses and sat down next to Joey in silence, looking for all the world like some exotic Chinese movie star. Joey was trying to be polite but he was also trying to carry out his uncle's orders, and this little bit of Chinese champagne wasn't part of the programme.

There was a long pause while he tossed up what to say. 'I'm here on business,' he said at last.

'So am I,' replied Simone.

'Yeah, well, if we meet anyone,' said Joey, 'I'm your friend Rocco and I'm a fucking bricklayer.'

Simone looked at Joey. 'Rocco the bricklayer. Got it,' she said.

God, thought Simone, this guy has to be, without a shadow of a doubt, the dumbest dago in the whole wide world, but he had a powerful brute force about him with an edge of evil to it. She couldn't help but feel physically attracted to the dumb thug. She couldn't really explain why she was attracted, but there it was. The 'Rocco the bricklayer line' was probably close to the truth – as if a size-10 IQ like this could possibly work for the Aspanu outfit, let alone be related to the old Godfather himself. She smiled to herself as she took Joey's hand. 'Rocco the bricklayer, that's easy to remember, babe.'

'Just make sure you do,' said Joey, then he looked directly at her tits under the cheesecloth shirt. Real smooth bastard. 'I thought you Chinese chicks were all flat-chested?' he remarked politely, just to keep the conversation going.

'My mother was Spanish Filipino,' replied Simone, puffing herself up, quite delighted by the fact her big tits had caught Joey's attention. A business-management degree got her in the corporate door, but her looks had helped her get her legs up the ladder. Whores stood on sidewalks and did it for peanuts; Simone didn't stand on sidewalks and, when she did the business, deals got done and million-dollar contracts got signed, and she worked not only on a salary but also on a commission bonus.

She might be the daughter of a Chinese pickpocket, but Simone was only one more good contract away from being a millionaire herself. No one called a rich girl a whore even if she looked like one.

As the two sat in the early-afternoon sunlight, a man walked towards Simone. Joey recognised him and glanced away, deadpan. It was Bruno Dietrich and Joey had something in his pocket for Bruno that was quite different from the thing he had in his pocket for Simone. One was .22 calibre; the other was rather bigger.

But any plans Joey had right then went out the window when Simone smiled and greeted Dietrich with a warm hello.

The first thing any Sicilian criminal is taught is that there is no such thing as a coincidence, and the lesson wasn't lost on Joey. He meets Simone Tao on a plane to Rome then he meets her again at the Rosati Cafe in the Piazza del Popolo. Now Simone is waiting for the same man his uncle wants hit.

Joey might not have been a heavy thinker, but he was fast. He decided to kill them both. Meanwhile, Simone was introducing Rocco the bricklayer to her friend Bruno the banker.

'German, hey?' said Joey, all smiles.

'No, Swiss,' said Bruno. 'Swiss German.'

Bruno Dietrich put on a thin false smile and Joey knew his Uncle Hector was right. He's a Swiss Jew. He had the right man. They chatted and drank coffee.

The hot sun belted down on the Piazza del Popolo but inside the church of Santa Maria del Popolo it was quiet and cool. A few rubbernecks wandered quietly about inside and an old priest was posing next to a statue of the Madonna for some Dutch tourists with a camera. Bruno Dietrich, Simone Tao and Joey Gravano walked in quietly. Bruno seemed excited.

'They have a hidden secret tunnel that leads to an underground crypt,' he said. 'I discovered it two years ago. Hardly anyone knows about it.'

Bruno Dietrich was meant to be transferring money from a numbered account in Switzerland to an account with the Royal Hong Kong Trading Company. Simone Tao had been sent to make sure the Royal Hong Kong Trading Company was well represented. If Dietrich needed to be encouraged via the bedroom, she would not only do the business with the contracts and transfers but also act as the Royal Hong Kong Trading Company's high-grade hooker. If the client wanted it that way she was ready, but she hadn't prepared herself for a guided tour of some ancient underground grave.

Simone didn't like graveyards and funerals. For that matter, in spite of her Catholic mother, she felt out of place in a church. Especially dressed in a pair of short pants that left little to the imagination, especially the imagination of the priest, whose eyes started bulging when he looked her way.

'For God's sake, I don't like graves,' she said.

' Don't worry,' replied Bruno soothingly. 'It's quite safe, all solid marble and granite. It won't cave in. It's of wonderful historical interest.'

Joey smiled and took her hand. 'It's OK, cheeky chops, I'm with ya. It's only an old grave, no ghosts,' he said. Not yet, he thought to himself. But there soon will be.

Bruno led the way to a side door and a staircase going down, then pushed at a painted wall that opened and the three walked through. Bruno turned on an electric light.

Joey grunted. 'What all secret chambers need. Electricity.'

Bruno didn't miss the sarcasm, and bit back. 'I said few people knew. I didn't say it was totally unknown.'

He wouldn't have been so cheeky if he'd known what was really going on. As Bruno led the way down another narrow stairway to the level below, Joey pulled out one of the things in his pocket: a neat .22-calibre magnum revolver. He produced a silencer and screwed it on the threaded end of the short barrel.

It's not like in the movies. Silencers don't make a spitting noise. When they're fitted to any gun, from a .22 calibre to a .44, they all make the same sound, like a high-powered air rifle going off, or the sharp clap of two hands smacked together. Not all that silent at all, but a hundred times quieter than any gun not fitted with a silencer.

Murder was never thrilling or mysterious. It was all very simple. The finger pulled the trigger, the bullet left the barrel and a small spot appeared in the back of Bruno's skull. He fell forward down the stairs. Joey pushed Simone forward and she stumbled down and fell on the body of the now dead Bruno.

She put her hands together as if in prayer, then began to beg. 'Please, please don't kill me, I won't say anything, I don't know what's going on, I don't know anything. Please, Rocco.'

'My name's Joey,' he said coldly.

She knew the moment he'd pulled the trigger that who he

said he was on the plane when they first met was correct. Bricklayers didn't tend to shoot Swiss bankers.

'Why shouldn't I finish you?'

Simone decided not to insult Joey with the promise of sexual heaven. A head job might get you out of a parking ticket in Italy, but it didn't carry much weight with mafia hitmen.

'The Chinese have a saying,' said Simone quietly. 'In return for a life you win a life.'

Joey looked puzzled.

Simone continued, 'If you give me my life today I will then give you my life. I will become yours to command with blind loyalty and obedience. I will owe my life to you, and it is a debt that I will spend the rest of my life repaying.'

In chess terms she had just placed him in check. A clever move. She had turned her own death into a matter of negotiation. A smart and level-headed lady.

Simone was nearly pooing her shorts in fear, but she could see Joey thinking about the old Chinese saying she had just invented, and she reminded herself that this particular Sicilian wasn't all that bright. Thank God.

Then Joey put the gun away and said, 'Get up, China.'

'You're letting me go?' she asked.

'Yeah, why not?' said Joey. 'You speak English, but you don't speak Italian. Italian police speak little English if at all and no fucking Chinese whatsoever. Think about it. A Chinese girl with your looks trying to report the murder of a German Swiss Jew carried out by the nephew of Hector Aspanu ... by the time you find an Italian policeman in Rome who speaks English, let alone Chinese, I'll have made a phone call and not only will Bruno here vanish but you'll also find two fat bags of pure heroin in your hotel room when the police take you back there. You with me so far, babe?' It wasn't really a question.

Joey was right: she was hardly in a position to report she had just witnessed a mafia execution, even if she was by nature or personality given to reporting things to police. Joey went up the stairs and Simone followed her new best friend like a little girl lost and found again. Extreme fear followed by extreme gratitude will do that. It's the Stockholm Syndrome. Ask Patty Hearst.

CHAPTER 3

LITTLE WOLF IN LONDON

London, 1992. Joey Gravano roared laughing at his own joke, as usual. This time it was the old cornflakes gag. Raquelle Jackson and Leon Little Wolf sat with him in London's famous Paul Raymond's Revue Bar, a nightclub and striptease palace.

Raquelle 'Action' Johnson was an Aussie film-maker who said she was doing a documentary on London's nightlife. In fact, she was secretly planning to expose mafia involvement in London's clubland, which was full of drugs and prostitution.

Leon Little Wolf was an American who had invested heavily in London's club scene. He was flattered by the fact Miss Johnson wanted to include him in her documentary, and feeling quite happy about things. Raquelle wasn't quite so happy. She was dubious about the thug from Carlton,

Melbourne, via Sicily, who had introduced himself as Rocco the bricklayer.

Raquelle knew the Melbourne crime scene and Rocco the bricklayer looked to her a hell of a lot like Aussie Joe Gravano, a person of interest to the authorities in more than one murder investigation and at least one Royal Commission she could think of. She recalled the name and the face popping up several times during the Trimbole investigation. Despite her uneasy feelings, she knew her documentary could be a winner if she could get a bit of secret footage of Gravano and Little Wolf together. Which is why she burst out laughing at the corny cornflakes joke as if she'd never heard it before. She knew that the Aussie Joe she'd heard of had only two social interests: playing chess and telling stupid jokes. She wondered if she could con him into a game of chess. She'd let him win, of course.

It was at this point that a big blonde stripper walked up to their table wearing a high-cut thong bikini bottom, a pair of stiletto heels, a wide smile and nothing else.

'Hi ya, Rocco,' she said in an East End accent.

'How's it going, Katrina?' said Joey, sticking some £20 notes down the front of the stripper's bikini. At least three, as Raquelle quickly counted.

The big blonde girl smiled even wider and, as if she had been through the same routine a hundred times before, she slid in beside Joey and started grappling with his crotch under the table.

God, thought Raquelle, she's going to do a Monica

Lewinsky right here at the table, and she hasn't even got a cocktail dress to wipe up the mess. Raquelle, a copper's daughter and a good girl at heart, who preferred her sport to be of the outdoors variety, was horrified at the very idea. But Leon Little Wolf seemed highly delighted.

Raquelle tried to avert her gaze, but in spite of her finer feelings she turned her head ever so slightly to see the stripper making a brave attempt on a thing the size of a hammer handle. That was enough for her. She got up.

'I'm going, Leon,' she said to the American.

Little Wolf, reluctant to pull himself away from what he was watching, decided to be the gentleman. 'Hang on, Raquelle,' he said. 'I'll see ya back to the hotel.'

As the American got up to leave, Joey cocked an eye on him, which wasn't a bad effort considering the advanced stage Katrina had reached in the mouth-to-south caper.

'Betorelli's, tomorrow lunchtime,' Joey said.

'Gotcha,' replied Leon.

Raquelle took a mental note of this as she walked out with Little Wolf, glad to turn her back on the stripper's little earner.

Raquelle knew enough about London to know that Betorelli's was a restaurant opposite the stage door of the Royal Opera House. While the rich and famous paid a small fortune to dine at the Savoy Grill in Covent Garden for food that tasted like deep-fried trash, Betorelli's served traditional Italian food. It was a favourite eating place for opera-goers and visiting mafia figures and it didn't cost the earth, unlike most other eateries in London, where customers would be as well off to be robbed with a stocking mask and a shotgun when they got in the door. In fact, many a tourist leaving a London restaurant imagined it might have been cheaper to cop an armed robbery than to eat out. One of the main offenders was Rule's Restaurant in Covent Garden, a quaint olde-worlde joint that served rabbit stew on Royal Doulton to prats in tweed jackets, then charged them like wounded buffalos. The grouse was grouse at Rule's, all right, but the price tag was enough for the deposit on a small country estate. Even the bloody ashtrays were worth half a week's wages, which was why so many of them were pinched by stray Aussie customers.

These were among the thoughts that raced through Raquelle's hyperactive mind as Leon drove her to Blakes Hotel, at 33 Roland Gardens. It wasn't her hotel. It was Leon who was staying at Blakes; Aussie documentary-makers generally stayed at the Abbey House or the Vicarage Hotel, relatively cheap but not bad. Raquelle was booked into the Vicarage but, tonight, in the name of journalistic endeavour, she had resigned herself to Blakes. The fact it was one of the plushest places in town, and one of the most expensive, wasn't the point. Raquelle knew what was ahead: she knew Mr Little Wolf wanted her to lie back and think of Melbourne while he attempted to tickle her fancy with something she was fairly sure wouldn't be in the same league as the Sicilian hammer handle she had just seen back at the nightclub.

Raquelle looked at Leon and said, 'Sorry, mate. I've changed my mind.'

'What's wrong, baby?' said Leon.

'Nothing,' said Raquelle, and handed him three £20 notes. 'I want you in my documentary — but ya can get that thing sucked elsewhere.'

She got out of the car and hailed a taxi. Leon looked at the £60 and shrugged, then turned the car around and headed back to the club. He most certainly would do as she suggested. No point wasting 60 quid.

Betorelli's restaurant, next day. Aussie Joe sat at a quiet window table with Leon Little Wolf.

'My friends are worried about the fucking gooks and their fucking heroin,' he said suddenly.

'Jesus, Joey,' replied Leon, 'you come to London to talk to me about fucking Chinese?'

'No, no. Not Chinese,' said Joey. 'Vietnamese. They're all over the place back home.'

'Australia,' said Little Wolf, pretending not to understand. 'You're talking to me as if I should know about what's going on in Australia.'

'Well,' said Joey, 'my uncle Hector seems to think you get on well with the Wong crew in Sydney.'

Leon stammered, 'The Wongs are Chinese.'

'Yeah,' said Joey drily, 'but the Viets sell China white smack. In the end, the Chinese control importation and the Viets work for them. We don't give a shit about fucking New South Wales. Just tell your little fat chow mate that the Viets in Melbourne work with us — or it's Irish time.'

'What do you mean?' asked Leon.

'Simple,' said Joey. 'We kill one Viet dealer Monday night, two Tuesday night, three Wednesday night, four Thursday night, five Friday night. We will turn Footscray into a Vietnamese graveyard.'

'Listen, Joey,' said Leon. 'I feel very uncomfortable with this conversation. Your uncle has it all wrong. Yes, I know Fat Micky – but knowing an Aussie triad boss socially don't mean I have any influence, for God's sake.'

Joey looked around. The place was crowded, but that didn't worry him much. Shooting a man in a crowded place was as good as a quiet place. The panic and shock means all anyone really remembers is the sound of the gun going off, then it's all eyes to the victim.

'So you can't have a word in a Chinese ear for my dear old uncle?' Joey asked sarcastically. 'They can do what the hell they like in bloody Cabramatta, but in Melbourne they play by the rules, that's all we ask.'

Leon put his hands in the air. 'This is insanity, Joey. I'm London-based. I have no influence whatsoever, for God's sake. Your uncle has fucked up on this one. Please believe me.'

Joey smiled as he drew his .38 police special under the table. 'My uncle is smart enough to know that Little Wolf Ltd invested six million with the Trantronic Australia Holding Company two weeks ago. Trantronic Australia is a Vietnamese group owned by the China Doll Toy company, Fat Micky's family firm.'

Leon went pale, and Joey knew the time had come to stop talking.

'Leon,' he said. 'We've had our main course; here's ya fucking dessert.'

He pulled the .38 out and pulled the trigger three times in Leon's face. The hollow-point ammo shattered inside the American's skull. A piece of lead spat out Leon's left ear, by which time he was extremely dead, although his body was twitching like a snake with a broken back. Joey was gone before the corpse hit the floor and the screaming started. He could move fast for a big man.

Raquelle Johnson whispered to her cameraman, 'Did ya get it, did ya get it?'

They had filmed the whole murder scene from a van parked a few feet from the window. All she'd wanted was film footage of the Aussie hood in London with the shadowy American, but this was much better. It was worth its weight in film awards.

'Let's get outta here,' Raquelle yelled to the driver. She couldn't contain herself. Any more excited and she was going to wet herself. A good exclusive was better than sex.

Raquelle sat in the first-class section of the British Airways flight from Heathrow to Melbourne. Her cameraman and film crew had somehow got themselves lost and missed the flight home. It was nearly breakfast time and Raquelle was feeling a touch peckish.

An air hostess approached her with a message. 'Miss Johnson?' she said enquiringly.

'Yes,' said Raquelle.

'I'm sorry, but there's been a little hiccup with your luggage.'

'What do you mean?' asked Raquelle, suddenly feeling ill at ease. The videotape was in her luggage. Why the hell hadn't she brought it in her hand luggage?

'What's the problem?' she asked.

'Oh, no problem really,' replied the hostess. 'We know where it is.'

'Well?' said Raquelle. 'Where is it?'

'Yes, well,' said the hostess, embarrassed. 'It somehow went from Heathrow to Gatwick Airport and, don't ask us how, ended up on a charter flight from Gatwick to – believe it or not, Miss Jackson – Palermo, Sicily. But don't worry. British Airways will compensate you fully if we can't recover it.'

She paused. 'What would you like for breakfast?' she asked lamely.

Raquelle had lost her appetite. She was stunned. Had she misjudged Aussie Joe? Maybe the dumb Sicilian killer wasn't the clown he pretended to be.

'What would you like for breakfast?' repeated the air hostess.

Raquelle looked up.

'I said,' repeated the hostess, 'what would you like for breakfast?'

Raquelle couldn't help laughing. 'Anything but the fucking cornflakes, honey. Anything but the cornflakes.'

Melbourne, 1978. Joey sat quietly with Pop Kelly over yet

another game of chess. 'What happened then, Mr Kelly?' he asked, after a longer than usual silence.

'What?' said Pop Kelly vaguely, trying to concentrate on the game.

'With ya dad?' asked Joey softly.

'Ya mean old Alfred Edgar Kelly, my dear old mad dad,' said Pop, laughing.

'Yeah,' said Joey, then moved his knight and said, 'Check.'

Old Pop quickly moved his king. 'During the '39–45 war or the '14–18 war? He fought in both,' said Pop.

'The First World War,' said Joey. 'The Pommy story.'

'Well,' said Pop. 'He turned 18 years old in France, got gassed seven times.'

'Nah,' said Joey. 'The Pommy captain.'

'Oh,' laughed Keith Kelly. 'Some la-di-dah, posh, anyone-for-fucking-tennis captain, Sir something-or-other, DSM, MBE, OBE – rah rah rah – came marching into the trench pissed, in the dead of night, and ordered the lads over the top. One of the chaps took offence at his tone and shot him stone dead, so the boys decided that after that the safest place was over the top so they all went over. Dad carried the body of the dead Pommy with him. They got 30 yards then the shooting started. This was the Western Front, son, dead of night. Mud, guts, blood and pissing down rain. The Aussies took a German trench and machine-gun nest.' Then he roared laughing.

'What's funny?' said Joey.

'The mad British top brass awarded the dead Pommy

captain a posthumous Victoria Cross for leading the bloody charge. Ha, ha, ha.'

The old bloke froze as Joey said the fatal words: 'Checkmate.'

Pop Kelly packed the chessboard away and stood up and held his hand out. Young Joey shook it, without really understanding what was going on.

'This is our last chess game, son,' said Pop Kelly.

'Why?' asked Joey.

'Well,' said Pop. 'I've learned nothing from beating you all these years, but, every time I've beaten you, in losing to me you have learned something. Ya see, son, when ya lose a game of chess, ya learn more than by winning. Slowly but surely, you have learned and remembered every move and counter-move, attack and defence, strategy and tactic. You now know all your teacher knows.'

Then Pop Kelly handed Joey an old book. 'Here ya go.'

'What's this?' asked Joey.

'It's a very rare book,' said Pop, 'written by Doctor Emanuel Lasker, who was one of the greatest chess masters in world history. Remember this, son, when you play chess with someone: they are showing you how to think tactically and strategically. Yes, the name of the game is not to win, but to learn. You must lose because the winner learns nothing, and the loser learns. Remember, chess is a lot like life. You might have to lose a thousand battles in order to win the war.'

Melbourne, 1989. Long before anyone in the western suburbs

ever heard of Quentin Tarantino, there was a game played in Footscray called the fantale game.

Niko Ceka, nicknamed Albanian Nick, sat at a large kitchen table in a small house. His cousin, a Russian Albanian called Fracoz Lepetikha and nicknamed Russian Frankie, sat with him. On the other side of the large wooden table sat Tony Capone, third-ranked member of Melbourne's Calabrian-controlled crime syndicate.

Tony didn't seem too pleased, as both his hands had been nailed firmly to the table. He had tears in his eyes but he wasn't crying. He was a tough hood. However, the mad Albanians in front of him dealt with tough guys for a living and to them Capone was just another punk dago who would soon be crying for his mother, a mother the Albanians might kill at a later date, anyway, just for practice.

They got up and walked around and stood either side of Capone. 'Now, Tony. We gonna play the fantale game.'

Tony didn't understand.

Niko produced a packet of fantales, a lovely-tasting chocolate lolly wrapped in yellow, blue and red wax paper. Each lolly paper contained a movie quiz question.

'OK, Tony,' said Niko. 'If you guess the name, you win. You guess wrong, you lose.'

Fracoz Lepetikha pulled out a razor-sharp butcher's knife.

'OK,' said Niko. 'First question. Born 5.1.31, he served in the US Army in Korea, on stage in Horton Foote's *The Midnight Call*. He began acting on television and appeared frequently in off-Broadway productions before making his screen debut as Boo Radley in the Gregory Peck film *To Kill a Mockingbird*.'

'Robert Duvall,' screamed Capone.

Niko looked at Fracoz in mock shock.

'That's all we need,' said Fracoz, 'a fucking dago movie buff.'

'Hang on,' said Niko, unwrapping another fantale. 'OK, OK, born in San Francisco 31.5.30, made film debut in *Francis in the Navy*, became a star in the spaghetti westerns *A Fistful of Dollars* and *The Good, The Bad and The Ugly*, introduced character Harry Callahan in the movie *Dirty Harry*.'

'Clint Eastwood!' yelled Tony Capone.

'Too easy,' sighed Fracoz. 'Even I knew that one.'

Niko opened yet another fantale and smiled. 'He won't get this one. Born Perth Australia, 1956. Catholic parents forbid her from seeing movies as a child. Joined an Italian band as a Blues singer and toured Asia. Returned to Australia to attend the National Institute of Dramatic Art.'

'Judy Davis,' yelled Capone.

Fracoz couldn't believe it. 'Jesus, Niko, this maggot must eat a truckload of bloody fantales. Find a hard one.'

Niko opened several more lollies and discarded them. Then he smiled wide. 'If he gets this one, ya can bend me over and screw me up the arse with a chainsaw,' he said by way of introduction. This passed for humour in Albanian crime circles.

'Born Demi Guynes 11.11.63 in New Mexico,' he started, before Capone interrupted, yelling, 'Demi Moore.'

Niko shook his head in disbelief. Capone was a bigger quiz king than Barry Jones.

'Who the fuck is Demi Moore?' asked Fracoz. 'C'mon, Niko, find one the rat won't guess. I don't believe this.'

'OK,' said Niko, rattling through the fantales like a loony.

'Son of actor Martin Sheen, began acting in theatre when he was 11.'

'Charlie Sheen!' yelled Capone, laughing. 'I've got you arseholes fucked.'

Niko smiled and nodded to Fracoz. 'Sorry, Tony, ya missed that one.'

'Bullshit!' yelled Capone. 'Charlie Sheen is the son of Martin Sheen.'

'Yeah,' said Niko, 'but so is Emilio Estevez.'

'Shit,' said Capone. 'I forgot about him.'

With that Fracoz took hold of the Italian's left ear and began slicing through it with the butcher's knife.

Capone screamed and the blood flowed like hot water. When the ear was off Fracoz put it in his pocket.

'Next question,' said Fracoz, an evil look on his ugly face.

Niko started again. 'Born New York City, 25.4.40, worked as small boy as usher and building superintendent, studied at Performing Arts New York Herbert Berghoff studio.'

'Al Pacino!' screamed Capone, now in tears.

'That's it,' said Niko. 'Cut his other ear off. If there's one thing I can't stand it's a fucking know-all. We pick the one dago in Melbourne who's a fucking film critic.'

Fracoz moved around and sliced the other ear off. It bled like a stuck pig. Fracoz put the second ear in his pocket and picked up a fantale and put it in his mouth and began to chew as Capone screamed.

'Joey only wanted the ears, didn't he, Niko?' asked Fracoz.

Niko nodded. He had a mouth full of chocolate.

'Then cut this arsehole's neck. All that crying will upset the neighbours.'

With that Fracoz slashed the Italian's throat with one lightning slice of the butcher's knife. Capone's head lolled backwards and air and blood bubbled and squirted all over the kitchen.

'Jesus,' said Niko, popping another lolly into his mouth, 'these fucking dagos bleed a lot.'

As Aussie Joe Gravano pulled up his car outside the small house in Herbert Street, Footscray, Fracoz and Niko walked out, still munching on fantales. Joey pressed a button and the driver's side window whirred down. Fracoz handed Gravano the ears.

'Jesus,' said Joey. 'Ya could have wrapped 'em in something.'

'We cut,' said Niko. 'We don't wrap. What do ya think we are, a fucking gift shop? Ya want ears, ya get ears. Ya want 'em wrapped, ya pay extra.'

Joey thought to himself that dealing with the Albanians was like dealing with the mentally ill.

'Ya want us to kill his mother as well?' said Fracoz.

'No, I don't want you to kill his mother. This is just to teach Tony a lesson. Now drop him off outside the Footscray Hospital.' He stopped, then added, 'He's staunch, he won't give no one up.'

Fracoz looked at Niko and Niko looked at Fracoz.

'What's wrong?' asked Joey. Then he realised. 'Jesus Christ, I said I wanted his ears, you fucking pair of lunatics. I didn't say kill him. I paid you fucking fruit loops $2000 each for his ears. Do you generally commit murder for $2000 each?'

Niko and Fracoz both looked at Joey and nodded.

'Jesus,' said Joey, 'no one kills no one for 4000 fucking dollars. This is fucking 1989, for God's sake.'

'Well,' said Niko, puzzled and a little put out, 'what should we charge?'

This question made Joey stop for a moment. The going rate for a hit was between $10,000 and $20,000, but these mad Albanians would kill anyone for sixpence.

Joey smiled. 'I want you two boys to work for me now full-time, but no more killing no one for $4000. From now on $6000 — that's $3000 each.'

Niko looked at Fracoz and smiled.

'But ya gotta dispose of the body as well,' added Joey.

'For $3000 each,' said Fracoz, 'that goes without saying.'

As Joey drove away Niko and Fracoz waved him goodbye.

'Three thousand each,' mused Fracoz. 'We're in the money now. In Albania anyone would kill anyone for $100 American and consider themselves very well paid.'

Australia was indeed the land of opportunity for young migrants prepared to work hard and make a go of things.

CHAPTER 4

RUSSIAN
ROULETTE

You're only 29, you've got a lot to learn.
And when your mummy dies she won't return.

Pentridge Prison, 1990
'The vilest deeds, like poison weeds, bloom well in prison air,
It is only what is good in man, that wastes and withers there,
Pale anguish keeps the heavy gate, and the warder is despair.'

Mirak Dardovski recited the Oscar Wilde classic *The Ballad of Reading Gaol* as he walked out of the jail that had been his home for quite a while. Mirak was an Australian-born Albanian who preferred to be called Mark Dardo. He was self-educated and loved the English and Aussie poets and would often recite Banjo Paterson or Kipling.

Dardo stood in front of the old bluestone prison, the College of Knowledge, or 'the ear factory', depending on your point of view. The warlords and tactical masters of ultra violence, the godfathers of insanity, lived behind those walls.

In matters of blood and violence Mark Dardo had been educated by the master of mental illness himself, Michael Brendon Kelly, the smiling chess master of strategy and psychological warfare. The same man who had given Mark his love of poetry.

Niko Ceka and Fracoz Lepetikha got out of a Ford LTD and yelled greetings in Albanian.

The three men were cousins, which was the same as brothers in Albanian culture. First, second and third cousins, uncles, brothers-in-law – they were all sons to the head of the Albanian clan. The Albanians lived by an honour code of blood loyalty. That's why the KGB picked all their hitmen from the mountain villages of Albania: they were bred for the job after generations of blood feuds.

Killing people was second nature to them. The idea of actually being paid money for it was a modern, western world idea that had great appeal. Still and all, for a friend, they would still kill for nothing. Money was a bonus.

Mark Dardo was pleased to see his cousins, but he wasn't too impressed with the fact they were now working for Sicilian Aussie Joe Gravano. Mark had nothing against Gravano personally, but he hated his Calabrian underlings. The Calabrians made trouble for the Albanian's underlings – the Little Cousins, as they called Romanians.

The Romanians in turn controlled the Yugoslavs and the Lithuanians. Dardo knew that Gravano's agreement with the Albanians would continue right up until their real friends told them to turn on their employers.

Niko put his foot down and the V-8 growled lazily as they sped away from Pentridge. Dardo considered the mad mosaic of internal politics that made up the criminal world of the maddest city in Australia, the city he loved so much. He thought of the friend he'd left behind in Pentridge, Michael Brendon Kelly. Then he burst out laughing.

'What's up?' asked Fracoz, grinning a bit but not understanding.

'I'm outta jail,' replied Mark. 'Can't a bloke have a giggle?'

Fracoz smiled and said nothing. His cousin was a criminal mastermind and a mental case. Who was he to question him?

'Micky Kelly wants us to shoot Aldo Gaspari on our way home,' said Mark suddenly, as if it had just occurred to him. 'Can we fit that in?'

'No problem,' replied Niko. 'He lives up here in Sydney Road.'

'I mean,' said Mark politely, 'is it on our way?'

'No worries,' said Niko. 'It's no trouble.'

Fracoz already had his gun out.

'Isn't he Gravano's brother-in-law?' asked Niko.

'Yeah,' said Mark. 'Is that a problem?'

'No,' said Niko. 'We don't work for Gaspari. We work for Gravano.'

Mark interrupted. 'No, Niko. You only pretend to work for Gravano. Remember that. You pretend to work for Gravano.'

Fracoz smiled. He was glad the brains of the crew was back.

Micky Kelly's simple request to shoot Aldo Gaspari was to Dardo a favour for a friend – but to Kelly it was all part of the chess game he was playing for the fun of it from inside his cell. Insane, but brilliant.

Gaspari wasn't at home at the Sydney Road address, but the three Albanians located him at the Regio Calabria Club in West Brunswick, not far away. Fracoz went inside with his Israeli-made .50-calibre action express automatic, a massive piece that would drop a charging elephant at a hundred yards. Mark and Niko sat in the car outside.

Four ear-splitting blasts rang out, and Fracoz ran out and jumped in and Niko hit the road.

'Did ya get him?' asked Mark.

'Dead as a door nail,' said Fracoz, looking a bit worried.

'What's the problem?' asked Niko.

'He was with his wife and mother-in-law,' said Fracoz.

'So,' asked Niko.

'So I shot 'em all,' said Fracoz.

'Jesus,' replied Niko.

'Gravano's sister and his mother. Fuck it, piss on 'em all,' said Mark Dardo. 'Gravano won't know who did it and, even if he finds out, if it came to a war between the Albanians and the dagos, we'd win it in an hour.'

But, as they drove away, they privately wondered if Mad Micky Kelly had just launched them into a gang war. They didn't worry too much, because they followed the credo that it's better to die in the name of a friend than to live in the name of an enemy.

The war between the Calabrian-Sicilian crews and the Albanian-Russian teams was something both sides knew would come. Kelly had just lit the fuse. Now it was up to the Albanians to toss the bomb in the right direction. Mark had to laugh to himself.

'Kelly, you cunning mental case, you'll be the death of us all. Ha ha.'

Sicily, 1990. Don Hector Aspanu sat in his humble two-room apartment in Palermo, with the telephone to his ear listening to his nephew Joey Gravano crying over the phone as he explained the murders of his mother, sister and brother-in-law.

'I can't prove it, Uncle Hector, but I think it's the fucking Albanians.'

'What have those animals got against Gaspari?' asked Uncle Hector.

'Nothing,' said Joey, 'but Mad Micky Kelly has a war going with the Calabrians and it smells as if he's behind this.'

'Fuck Gaspari,' said Uncle Hector. 'I told your sister not to marry a fucking Calabrian. They're no good for anything except getting killed at the wrong time.'

Joey rambled on wildly. 'This is war, Uncle.'

'Yes,' said Hector. 'It is war. But you take no part.'

'What?' gasped Joey.

'You come back to me now,' Hector said. 'Now, I'll handle

it all, OK? I don't want you in some insane war with madmen in Melbourne.'

'But, Uncle!' cried Joey.

'Shut up!' yelled Hector. 'You're on the next plane out of there.' He slammed down the phone.

Joey sat in the lounge of his home in Carlton. This was a nightmare. Micky Kelly was the insane son of old Keith Kelly, the swimming instructor, his old chess master. Kelly's influence over the tactical thinking of the Albanian criminal clans via Mark Dardo was unbreakable. Joey knew that a blood war face to face with the Albanian clans was suicide. His revenge had to be cold, secret and silent. Uncle Hector was a master of silent revenge. He must obey his uncle. Rage boiled up in him, but he knew logic and business must rule. Uncle Hector would handle it.

To act hastily is what Kelly wanted. But before Joey went home to Sicily he would arrange for a bomb to be placed under the hood of Pop Kelly's car and a funeral wreath to be delivered to the old man's door. At least Michael Brendon Kelly would know that the Sicilians realised he was behind the Albanian move and that he would not be forgotten.

Yes, he must obey his uncle Hector. It was smart. But, deep in his heart, Joey couldn't help feeling like a coward. Business and survival had become more important than honour. How long could the mafia survive with that attitude? Did the future truly belong to the money men and the criminal financial brains — or to the mindless warring tribes? Uncle Hector was right about the rest of the world, but Joey wasn't so sure about Melbourne. It still belonged to the warring clans. Joey Gravano was a hitman, not a gang-war strategic tactician, but he was deeply disturbed. The old, dark Sicilian way had placed family honour, revenge, the vendetta and loyalty to the brotherhood above all else. But since the 1970s money, business and long-term survival had replaced the old Sicilian and Calabrian code of blood for blood at any cost. Since then it had mostly been a case of, if it wasn't worth it, walk away and deal with it another time. Why destroy an empire in a war you can't win, over a few dead relatives?

Blood had been the oil that kept the whole mafia machine running and, without the threat of it, that beautiful money-making machine might just seize up and be replaced by some group that was prepared to be more ruthless.

He remembered the old chess master, Doctor Emanuel Lasker, and his doctrine of allowing the other side to attack and then using that attack against them, and in doing so isolate the king. This was the real thing, a game far more evil and treacherous and dangerous than a board game – but the principle still applied. He must allow the enemy to think him a fool or a coward and in doing so control the game by using the other side's attack as his greatest weapon. It was, after all, known as the Sicilian Defence.

France, 1991. Big Al Guglameno, Little Anthony Capone, Eddie Giordano, Tommy Monnella, Fat Sally Gigante, Little Boy Bobby Aspanu and Sammy Gravano, little brother of

Aussie Joe, all sat at a table by a pool in the rear yard of a luxury villa in the French Riviera.

Aussie Joe was in Paris. There had been a shooting at the airport of two New York mobsters on their way to attend the meeting at the quiet villa on the Riviera. What the Sicilians and Calabrians at the meeting were pondering privately was that one of their own number may be an informer. Aussie Joe had met with his own informer in the drug enforcement administration at the Jules Verne restaurant on the Eiffel Tower. He had left that meeting in shock at what he'd been told, then proceeded to the Moulin Rouge nightclub to meet yet another source of dubious information. Then he went to the Crazy Horse and Harry's Bar. It was a big night, but for once Aussie Joe wasn't enjoying himself.

After returning to his hotel, he rang his uncle Hector. He couldn't believe what his contacts had told him, and he wanted to talk about it.

Gorgeous George Marcus wasn't a 24-carat gold hood. He was more a criminal yuppie, a fetch and carry boy. No one really trusted him, but he was eager to please and did what he was told. Every culture has its hangers-on and Gorgeous George loved to mix with gangsters. He believed he was part of it all. Big Al Guglameno, the Carlton-born Calabrian, used Marcus as a lackey and, in return, Marcus was allowed to live out his gangster fantasy – borrow money and not repay it, threaten people and get away with it, and in general act the role of the gangster playboy. When Big Al wanted a girl he'd send George to fetch him one. He was good at that bit.

The poolside meeting was interrupted when gorgeous George walked into the courtyard with a tall, awesome-looking German girl. She was spectacular, all long legs and tits. How the hell George found such gorgeous creatures was a never-ending source of amazement to Big Al.

The big beautiful blonde German was evidently an air hostess on a hitchhiking holiday around France. The Germans' love of backpacking saw German girls murdered and raped all over the world. The fact that this beauty had agreed to get into George's car, return with him to the villa to stand in front of this evil group of gangsters beaming a big smile, wearing short shorts and a tight T-shirt, mountain-walking boots and a look in her large blue eyes of total delight was proof to all gathered that German backpackers were either all mentally retarded, suicidal or nymphomaniacs.

Her name was Helga and she was welcomed with wide smiles and a line of cocaine that would have killed any normal woman. The only effect it seemed to have on Helga was to make her feel the need to disrobe herself. Having removed her boots, socks, shorts, panties and T-shirt, she dived into the pool, with Big Al Guglameno and little Anthony Capone close on her heels.

'Jesus Christ,' said Sammy Gravano. 'Don't they have any cocaine in fucking Germany?'

'You dirty bastard,' yelled Tommy Monnella to Little

Anthony. 'Don't screw her in the pool – people gotta swim in that after you.'

A rumble of general agreement followed this, regarding hygiene.

Helga didn't seem to care. She was hanging on the edge of the pool with her arse aimed in Capone's direction. Capone couldn't contain himself, and with his hands holding on to the massive tits for support he went for it.

'You dirty bastard!' yelled Sammy Gravano.

Big Al Guglameno got out of the pool.

'Where did ya find this nutcase?' he asked George Marcus.

'Just hitchhiking, all tits and arse and waving it about.'

'I don't know how you pull 'em,' said Big Al to Marcus, shaking his head, 'but every time you produce a chick she's a bigger raving rat than the last one.'

George Marcus smiled at this compliment.

'Correct me if I'm wrong, Anthony,' said Tommy Monnella to Little Anthony. 'But I think ya Nazi girlfriend is having some sort of heart attack.'

'Anthony likes to finish what he starts,' said Big Al.

Capone let out a cry and a shudder, then got out, leaving the German backpacker quietly sinking to the bottom.

'Well,' said Sammy Gravano, 'I'm definitely not going swimming till we've had the pool cleaned.

'George, you brought the moll here. You can dump her – and next time bring us a healthy one,' Sammy continued. 'I've never seen anything so disgusting in all my life. This is supposed to be a fucking holiday. Get the pool emptied and clean it up, George. You brought her here, you get rid of her.'

'I think it was the cocaine,' said Marcus mildly.

'Three grams of pure coke in a giant fat line,' growled Sammy. 'Ya wouldn't need to be a rocket scientist to work that out.'

Aussie Joe Gravano returned to the villa the following day to find all the boys sitting around a now empty swimming pool. Aussie Joe had something on his mind.

For some time he had suspected Big Al and his crew of two-bob Calabrian offsiders. He'd given them the task of putting the bomb in Pop Kelly's car, and that had turned into a fuck-up. Guglameno had neglected to include a detonator. So there were six sticks of gelignite all wired up to the ignition and no detonator.

Old Pop Kelly found the bomb and, being of the old school who hated waste of any sort, he carefully saved it up, got a detonator and two weeks later the same bomb was used by Micky Kelly's insane Jewish offsider Mad Benny Shaprio to blow the arse out of the Calabrian Social Club in North Fitzroy.

It was a thing of beauty, that explosion. Especially when stupid Guglameno promptly blamed the Yugoslavs for it. In a gang war Big Al wouldn't know if you were up him with an arm full of chairs. As far as blood and guts strategy and tactics went, he was so far behind he couldn't hear the band playing, but he was a good drug dealer and money mover.

When suspicions were raised about a double agent in the

camp, Aussie Joe secretly hoped it would be Guglameno, but he thought he knew the truth was otherwise, and it made him downhearted.

Uncle Hector had cleared it and Aussie Joe had been given his orders. There was no turning back. For Don Hector the leaked information about who the informer was came as no surprise, and he knew exactly what had to be done.

Aussie Joe was part of a hard clan, perhaps not quite as mindless as the worst Irish and Albanians, but when it came to the old Sicilian ways concerning honour and revenge the Aspanu clan had harder rules for their friends and family than they appeared to have for their enemies in business. A strange contradiction of the Sicilian personality is that they expect to be attacked by their enemies – that is business – but betrayal by friends and family is considered far worse because it is personal.

Enemies in war and business can only really stab you in the arse, but the betrayal of a loved and trusted friend or family member is a stab to the heart …

This explains why Aussie Joe Gravano walked into the courtyard in stony silence, ignoring loud and warm greetings from the men gathered there. He shook hands and embraced and kissed each man, then embraced his little brother Sammy last of all.

Anybody who was watching Joey closely would have noticed he had tears in his eyes, which wasn't exactly what they'd expect. He kissed his brother on the mouth and said quietly, '*Como Sardechi Questo in Siciliano*, Sammy?'

Sammy didn't fully understand the old Sicilian Scarchi slang dialect but the expression 'How do you say this in Sicilian?' was not lost on him. It meant how do you say death in Sicilian.

Joey was crying now, as Sammy stammered for a reply.

The other Italians in the group could make out only every second or third word. Scarchi was a mountain Sicilian slang, an old dialect.

Then, without warning, Aussie Joe thrust an ice pick into the left ear of his young brother, into the brain. Sammy's eyes closed and as Joey withdrew the ice pick Sammy fell like a rag doll to the marble floor. The other men stood in silence. They realised Sammy must have been an informer. They knew one Sicilian doesn't kill another, let alone his own baby brother, unless family honour and orders from the head of the family are involved.

No man spoke. They filed out of the courtyard, leaving Aussie Joe crying as he stood over his brother's body.

Joey went down on his knees over the body of his fallen brother, crossed himself and said a short prayer in Latin.

There were a few tough Italians in that group that day, but each man left the villa with a new sense of respect, and the chilling thought that he stood with one foot in the grave if he fucked up.

Gorgeous George Marcus made the call to the National Crime Authority headquarters in Melbourne. He was talking to Julian Farrance, QC, deputy director of the organised crime unit.

'I'm telling ya, Julian, his own fucking brother!' he chortled down the phone. 'Al is in the clear. All it takes now is for old Aspanu to give the nod and Poppa Di Inzabella will give Al the nod, then he controls it all in Melbourne. Gravano thought his own brother was the dog that wagged its tongue and not its tail. Ha ha.

'It went magic. The DEA trick worked an absolute treat, fair dinkum. These fucking Sicilians are too busy being paranoid to think clearly. Yeah, yeah, OK. I'll tell him. See ya.'

He hung up and returned to the car of Al Guglameno.

'All sweet?' asked Al.

'Yeah,' said George, still grinning.

Big Al never spoke to his police connections on the phone in case his voice was recorded. Likewise, he never met with them. He used George Marcus as his middle man with his NCA, DEA and Federal Police contacts. It had all been arranged by a lawyer friend of his who was now a judge.

George Marcus loved it. It made him feel like he was some sort of covert operation James Bond secret agent. What he didn't stop to consider was that, any time Big Al felt he needed to protect himself from being exposed, he only had to have poor simple George killed. The splendid legal system being what it is in a modern democracy, the police would have a hell of a time proving to anyone that Guglameno was their man, when all the time they had only ever dealt with Marcus. It was a tactic known in some circles as a version of the 'lemon twist'.

George Marcus was worth his weight in jelly beans. To find

someone as stupid as George was good fortune indeed for Guglameno. And, after seeing what Sicilians did to their own family members suspected of being rats, Big Al appreciated George Marcus all the more.

CHAPTER 5

THE PAIN IN SPAIN

Them barber chaps what keep a tote,
By George I've had enough.
One tried to cut me bloomin' throat,
But thank the Lord it's tough.
BANJO PATERSON

Europe, 1991. While the rest of the crew flew home from Paris, Aussie Joe went to Spain to catch up with his old mate, the China doll Simone Tao.

Simone had proved herself a blood-loyal friend since 1987 and, having just butchered his baby brother, Joey thought attending a bullfight with Simone might cheer him up, although it was hard to say why watching Spaniards in fancy dress filleting a live bull would make him chirpy after his recent ice-pick trick, but that's Sicilian mobsters for you.

Aussie Joe tried to see Simone at least twice a year, and they both loved Spain. They'd take a beautiful apartment, have lunch at the Cafe Leon, dinner at the Casa Ciriaco restaurant, then on to a flamenco show. All very Christopher Skase, except that Aussie Joe paid his bills and didn't pretend to need a respirator.

However, the fine dining and cultural pursuits sometimes got postponed because Simone had proved a master of the sexual arts and Joe often found himself unable to leave the luxury apartment for some time.

Joe had to admit that Simone had a lot in common with a circus sword swallower and, although she spoke several languages, she hadn't mastered the word 'no'. She also had a little weakness for being smacked across her exquisite buttocks with a leather strap until she cried 'I'm sorry' for some imagined wrongdoing. But that was by the way. Simone had the brain of a pocket calculator and the loyalty of a one-owner hound dog, and Aussie Joe had come to like the twisted Chinese beauty.

He felt at ease and relaxed and less paranoid in her company, and so it was the two old friends sat in the Cafe Leon drinking Spanish coffee. Simone, with a few drinks in her, would let herself go and regale him with tales of her recent adventures on behalf of the Royal Hong Kong Trading Company.

This time, she told him of a recent business trip to Istanbul. She had to meet a Turkish general who, as it happened, was also a drug lord and merchant banker. It seems most Turkish generals have a second or third job that mostly involves either murder, prostitution or drugs.

Anyway, this particular general, Mustafa Manager, also claimed to be some sort of Turkish prince, and who was Simone to argue? She didn't give a shit for anything except the bottom line, a phrase with more than one meaning in Istanbul.

She was collected by a police car and taken to the Orient Express Bar at the Pera Palace Hotel. The night went well. The general handed Simone a list of numbers and coded names and accounts. He didn't trust the postal service, telephone, fax or email, and liked to do business by hand, face to face. The slow way, but generally foolproof.

Simone fully expected to be taken to bed by the general as part of the deal. She was wrong. It turned out that waiting for her upstairs was the general's esteemed grandfather, an old gentleman who'd never had a Chinese girl and was feeling curious.

The general, evidently very family-oriented, wanted to delight his grandfather's heart by supplying a beautiful Oriental girl. It seemed the good general himself preferred teenage boys. Which is why Simone found herself on her knees trying mouth-to-south resuscitation to the old boy's old boy. It seemed that in Turkey everyone went the gobble.

Despite her valiant attempts, it was a losing battle. The old Turk was in the Muslim version of heaven – but his equipment didn't want to work. It took Simone nearly an hour to arouse the old gentleman into a state where she could mount. He then seemed to rise to the occasion, but, just as he was getting to the funny bit, it all became too much. He went into some sort of convulsions. He was doing a Sir Billy Snedden – having a heart attack on the job.

Simone jumped off immediately and called the general. The old man was rushed to hospital, but there was no gratitude for her quick thinking. Simone spent three days in a military police cell being beaten and worse, until she was a mess at both ends. Meanwhile, the general's grandfather got better – so well that he asked after the delightful Chinese girl he'd been so kindly introduced to at the hotel.

You don't have to be told: Simone was rushed to hospital and bathed and pampered and provided with medical attention, then filled full of morphine. Two days later she was at the hotel again, on her knees doing the same trick that had caused all the trouble in the first place, praying the old bastard wouldn't drop dead on her. Her luck held. This time he didn't.

The result was that Simone swore Turkey was off her travel agenda. Through the friendship of Aussie Joe, she had been invited to Sicily to meet the great Don Hector Aspanu. The Aspanu Group had entrusted quite a large amount of money to the Royal Hong Kong Trading Company, which had rocketed Simone up the corporate ladder.

Don Hector was an old gentleman in some ways, and there was no sex involved whatsoever. He did, however, take her to see his favourite movie every time she visited Palermo. The

Don would hire the whole movie theatre so Simone could sit in the empty theatre with him and his two bodyguards and watch his favourite, the 1950s B-Grade classic *The Girl Can't Help It*, starring Jayne Mansfield ... all dubbed in Sicilian dialect, if you don't mind.

Simone had visited Don Hector five times and, between the Jayne Mansfield movie and the all-night poker games in which everyone was expected to lose to Don Hector, she felt quite at home. No one dared even suggest sex, let alone put any moves on her.

Evidently, a smile from Don Hector and a pat on the head with the comment of 'You're a gooda girl, Simone, I lika you' was enough to ensure she could walk through the red-light district of Palermo, swinging her arse like a bitch on heat and the local mad rapist would rather put a loaded gun in his mouth and pull the trigger than touch her.

Palermo was not a place where one saw a lot of Chinese girls and the Chinese lady who went to the movies with Don Hector had become a topic of whispered gossip and mystery.

Joey picked a pause in the story to break in. 'I need a haircut,' he said. 'Where the hell do ya find a barber's around this joint?'

Simone spoke to the waiter, then said, 'Two streets away. Only a short walk.'

'Yeah, well, let's go,' said Joey, 'and you can tell me some more funny stories on the way.'

Simone smiled and took his hand as they walked in the sunshine.

One would think that a Spanish barber shop would contain a Spanish barber, not a Greek who spoke English. But when Aussie Joe settled into the chair the barber introduced himself as Peter and said, 'Welcome to my shop. You English, I can tell.'

He was obviously addressing Joey, as Simone hardly passed as English.

'Italian,' grunted Aussie Joe, 'from Australia.'

'Ah,' said Peter the Greek. 'I have the relations in Australia.'

'What's their name?' said Joe despite himself, amazed at what a small world it was.

'Kravaritis,' said Peter the Greek.

Joe thought he'd try out some basic phonetic Greek on this funny so-called Greek barber as he cut his hair. '*Ya su ray te kunus ray.*' He had no idea how to spell Greek, but he knew a few choice phrases from his time on the streets.

Peter laughed, but replied in English, which Joe thought was odd.

'*Te kalla veno?*' asked Joe, meaning, 'Do you understand?'

The Greek laughed again, then Joe continued. '*Te mama su gar mussus ray.*'

The Greek laughed again. Joe had just used his worst broken Greek to suggest that the barber had sex with his own mother.

'*Pusti malaka ray,*' continued Joe.

The barber was about as bloody Greek as Simone was, thought Joe. He had just called him a poofter in Greek, and got no reaction at all.

After the haircut the barber was looking nervous. 'You want shave?' he asked.

Joe nodded and said something like '*ef kara stou*' meaning 'thank you', then blew the barber a kiss and said '*sarg a pau*' meaning 'I love you'.

The barber was now very nervous, but looked as if he had something on his mind. He certainly had something in his hand. It was a cut-throat razor.

'Kravaritis, hey?' said Joe loudly. 'Sounds Albanian to me. A lot of Albanian grandmothers got raped by Greeks.'

With that the barber slashed Joe across the neck. Joe held his throat with his right hand to preserve his vital spark as the blood rushed out, and went for his gun with his left hand.

'*Nay drobro draco bracho,*' said Joe in Albanian.

The barber understood that, but it didn't help him any. Joe fired a shot into his guts. As the barber dropped to his knees, Simone Tao, now armed with one of the cut-throat razors from the bench, walked up and slashed his neck from ear to ear. Then she helped the bleeding Gravano out of the shop and into a taxi. The driver was ordered to drive to the nearest hospital, as if he needed telling. Joe could still talk, which meant his windpipe was intact and his jugular vein unharmed.

'Was that a hit on you?' yelled Simone.

'How could it be?' said Joe, shaking his head – but not much, in case the wound bled worse. 'Just some paranoid insane Albanian hiding out in Spain not expecting to see an Aussie dago who spoke Greek and could tell the difference between a Greek and an Albo.' The expression Albo puzzled Simone, as it sounded like elbow.

'Albanian,' explained Joe. 'Ya only got to blink the wrong way in front of a paranoid Albanian and he will think you're out to kill him and will try to get in first. Of all the fucking barber shops in Spain, we walk into some hideout for mental-case Albanians.'

'Jesus Christ. You mean all that was sheer coincidence?' asked Simone incredulously.

Joe nodded. 'It's not so strange,' he said. 'I know barbers in Sicily who cut one neck a month because they don't like the colour of ya fucking tie. I think I'll cut my own hair from now on,' he added savagely as the taxi screamed to a halt outside a medical clinic.

The close call with the mad Albanian barber caused the police to raid the barber shop to investigate his death – only to find a heroin-processing factory operating in the back. They promptly forgot the murder to proudly boast to the media they had busted an Albanian mafia heroin ring in Madrid. According to the Spanish press, the Albanians worked for the Sicilian mafia.

Yeah, Joe thought when he heard that, when the bastards aren't trying to kill us they're working for us.

It was 1993. Franco Di Tommaso and Luigi Monza spoke no English but Little Boy Bobby Aspanu did. Bobby preferred it that way. When he went to Australia and got off the plane at Tullamarine Airport, as he did several times a year to visit friends and relatives in Melbourne, he always used Sicilian bodyguards who spoke no English.

Di Tommaso was a member of the Aspanu clan, but Monza wasn't. He was a member – or former member – of the outlawed Italian masonic lodge P2. If a candidate in the Italian craft failed a test or in a duty or obligation of trust or otherwise 'fucked up', he was either killed or, as with Monza, had the last joint on his right index finger cut off. This meant he could be identified in the dark or if he shook hands with any member of the lodge and immediately recognised as an outcast from the organisation.

The Aspanu clan offered Monza a safe haven, and his gratitude and loyalty to Little Boy Bobby Aspanu was without question.

On this trip Bobby was meant to be visiting his uncle Joey Gravano, but that was only an excuse for Bobby to see Alphonse Guglameno and his Calabrian crew – Eddie Giordano, Tommy Monnella, Little Anthony Capone – and Gorgeous George Marcus, the Greek who pretended to be Italian.

Bobby had other Melbourne interests. He was, for instance, screwing Tommy's little sister Sally Monnella. To Bobby, Sally had a lovely name. He couldn't work out why, in Australia, people found her full name so funny. These Aussies had an odd sense of comedy.

'My bloody uncle's had a bit of bad luck with his last two wives,' said Tina Torre to Joey Gravano.

'Yeah?' said Aussie Joe. 'What happened?'

'Well,' continued Tina, 'his first wife died after she ate some poison mushrooms.'

'Shit,' said Joey. 'What happened to his second wife?'

Tina was trying hard to keep a straight face. 'Well,' she said, 'she died from a blow to the back of the head with a claw hammer.'

'Fucking hell!' said Joey, totally convinced Tina was telling the truth. 'Who did that?'

'My uncle, actually,' she replied.

'Why?' asked Joey, still believing her wild yarn.

'Cos she wouldn't eat her bloody mushrooms, that's why' said Tina, bursting out laughing.

Joey went silent, then smiled and made a mental note to add that story to his endless list of jokes. The mushroom joke was as old as the hills but he hadn't heard it before.

The two sat in the lounge bar of Squizzy Taylor's Hotel in Fitzroy. Strictly speaking, this was enemy territory but they were waiting to meet Tina's best mate Cassandra Connor. The Connors were related to the McCall family and the Reeves and Pepper clans, the Browns, the Kellys, the Scanlans and the rest of the mad dogs who infested Collingwood, Fitzroy and Richmond. Tina Torre was a good girl with no involvement in the criminal world. She honestly believed Joey Gravano was a bricklayer. She had a kind face and a smile that would melt ice. If you took her home to meet your mother, your dad would fall in love with her. Joey had been raised on a diet of lowlife sluts and found Tina a welcome change. The only problem was that, while she had a face made in heaven, the devil had played a part in designing her body. She looked as if she were built for sin, which can tend to get a nice girl into trouble.

There was something about her that frightened Aussie Joe. On the one hand, when looking at her body, he wanted to drop his pants and do bad things. But, on the other hand, he had an overwhelming urge to say the fatal words 'I love you'. The truth was, he would marry Tina any time if he could only muster up the courage to ask her – but she was from another world.

To her, he was a bricklayer who owned his own business, dressed well, had a few bob and maybe got into a few Saturday-night punch ups. How could he ever marry this lovely young lady and say, 'I'll be back in three weeks, my darling, my uncle wants me to fly to Timbuktu and shoot a few people. Ya see, honey, as well as laying bricks I kill people for a living and the people I work for, and my enemies, would cut your head off if I ever fucked up too badly or dropped my guard.' Which is why Joey didn't declare his love for her.

As for Cassandra Connor, she was as mad as a cut snake, all legs and a scallywag grin that told you don't give this chick a match because she'd sure as hell burn your house down. Tina was fascinated in all she saw; Cassandra was amused in all she saw. Tina looked like a lady any man would want to protect; Cassandra looked like someone who'd front up for a crew wishing to sell protection.

Aussie Joe felt slightly ill at ease around young Cassie, but the two young ladies were the best of mates and Tina was one of the very few straight friends he had. For Joey, time spent with Tina and Cassie was rest and relaxation, even though Cassie could unnerve him with a twinkling eye and cheeky grin that said, 'If you're a bricklayer, I'm a bloody Irish brain surgeon.'

Cassie Connor walked into the bar carrying a brand-new birdcage. 'Hi ya, Cass,' said Tina.

'Hi, Tina,' said Cassandra.

'What's the birdcage for?' asked Joey.

'I'm gonna put me fucking cat in it, ya bloody spazzo,' she answered tartly.

Joey ignored the insult and looked at the cage for a moment before realising she had no intention of putting her cat in it at all. The question was begging: why she was carrying an empty birdcage. She had either lost her bird or was on her way to collect one or was taking the new cage home to replace an old cage. Joey decided not to ask. Italian logic versus Irish-Aussie comedy always made him look dumb.

Joey looked back at the empty cage. He couldn't help himself. 'Seriously, Cassie. What's it for?' But she didn't tell him.

Later that night, Joey walked Tina home hand in hand, long after crazy Cassie had vanished into the darkness with her empty birdcage.

Tina lived in a block of flats in Gertrude Street and, as was their routine, they stood on the footpath in front of the flats and had a little goodnight cuddle like a pair of teenagers. Joey put his arms around Tina and she wrapped her arms around him and they kissed. Tina slid her tongue into his mouth in a way that sent an electric shock through him and he wondered desperately if she noticed the massive bulge in his pants. Tina wasn't quite as slow on the uptake as her virgin face implied. This time, she grabbed hold of the swelling and said with mock seriousness, 'Ya know, Joey, ya gonna have to see a doctor about that lump of yours.'

Joey couldn't help himself this time. He reached his hands down and took hold of Tina's round firm arse. She had her arms around his neck and her already short skirt had crept up and Joey could feel warm flesh. She was wearing high-cut knickers, naturally, and he found he had his hands full of silky-smooth arse cheeks and she still had hold of him. This was right in the middle of Gertrude Street, Fitzroy. The tongue-kissing had got serious by this time. Then both of Tina's hands went south.

Joey was trying to get into the shadows under the flats. His hands had slipped under her knickers. Neither of them had planned this but both knew that in about 30 seconds something of a seriously passionate nature was about to happen.

Joey lifted her up. She wrapped her legs around his waist and her arms around his neck. But the thing she wanted most was still in his pants, so, while little Tina hung on with her tongue running in and out of his mouth, Joey fumbled frantically. Tina lifted her hips up, knowing Joey needed a little help to direct the head of the problem into the mouth of the solution. Then, with a few little jiggles up and down, Tina sank her hips down with a moan.

Who said romance was dead? She began to ride him up and down, hanging on to his neck for dear life. 'I love you, Tina,' he said urgently. 'I love you.'

That's what Tina wanted to hear. Her passion seemed to go from smouldering to red hot and she replied with a frantic effort to get as much of Joey into her as she could. All of a sudden, Tina wanted to pop this guy's weasel so badly nothing else mattered.

Tina was moaning and riding him like it was the first and last time in her life. Suddenly, they heard something like a car backfiring three times. A piece of the brickwork behind Joey shattered off and hit Tina in the neck. The next thing she knew she was on the ground, staring in horror at Joey pulling out a gun with one hand and putting his other weapon away with the other. He had blood on the side of his face, not from a bullet but from flying brickwork. The three gunshots hadn't hit home but they'd come close. Joey ran into the street and fired five shots at a bashed-up old Ford as it sped off.

When he returned Tina had found her feet, but not her temper.

'What was that all about?' she demanded.

'Ah, just some blokes who don't like me,' said Joey carefully.

'You're not a bricklayer, are ya, Joe?'

'Nah, Princess, I'm not.'

'Then what the hell are you?' said Tina.

'Just a good bloke out of luck, Princess, just a good bloke out of luck.'

As they walked upstairs to Tina's flat, she was full of fear, fascination and questions.

'Do ya really love me, Joey?'

'Yeah, darlin', I do. I always have, in fact. I just never had the guts to tall ya.'

Tina hugged him. 'Ya big dummy, you should have said something.'

Joey continued, 'We come from different worlds, Princess. I didn't want to get you involved in my life.'

'But I am involved, Joey. That's what love is, you and me against the rest of the world. That's love,' said Tina.

They laughed as they went into Tina's flat to finish what the gunplay had so rudely interrupted.

While Tina Torre spent the rest of the night showing Joey Gravano just how bad a good girl could be, Little Boy Bobby Aspanu and his two shadowy Sicilian bodyguards sat in the Gangitano Lounge in Carlton. Big Al Guglameno, Eddie Giordano, Tommy Monnella and a big crew were all trying to convince Bobby Aspanu that the fuck-up on the attempted hit on his uncle Joey wouldn't come back on them.

'Bullshit,' said Bobby, 'only a fuckin' Calabrian would try shooting someone at night from a moving car with a handgun at a distance of 60 feet. Jesus, who do you think you are, Monnella? Roy fucking Rogers?'

Monnella looked shamefaced. 'Gravano won't know it was us. He'll blame the Albanians,' he said.

THE PAIN IN SPAIN

Bobby Boy Aspanu laughed at this, but he didn't look amused. 'If the Albanians wanted to hit Gravano, they would get out of the car in broad daylight in front of a hundred witnesses and cut Gravano's head off with a meat axe,' he snarled. They all knew it was close enough to true.

'What about Kelly and the Aussie crews?' said Giordano.

Guglameno answered this one. 'They would run into him in a pub and take his head off with a shotgun. Overalls, gloves, balaclava, getaway car. Cop this, Joey. Bang. Bobby's right, Gravano will know we tried it.'

Little Boy Bobby got up to leave. 'It's like the old song, isn't it, boys? Clowns to the left of me, jokers to the right and here I am stuck in the middle with a bunch of dagos who couldn't run a three-seated shit-house without getting one of the pans blocked up.'

'Don't panic,' said Big Al soothingly. 'Joey will never jerry that it was you who gave the order.'

Secretly Guglameno knew that Gravano would know right away that no Calabrian crew would dare to make a move on him without a Sicilian order. The Calabrians were soldiers following commands. Which meant that Little Boy Bobby was the one in big trouble.

As Bobby walked out, Tommy Monnella couldn't help himself. 'She's sweet, Bobby. Ya grandfather will understand it's all business, mate. He knows that.'

The Calabrians looked at each other and smiled.

'Ya did good,' said Guglameno to Monnella. 'A dead Gravano is no use at all but an angry Gravano out for revenge is worth his weight in Sicilian blood. Let them animals kill each other. We run Melbourne. Those Sicilian cockroaches get off the plane two, three times a year and tell us what to do for 25 per cent of our action.'

Peter Della Torre, a Sicilian, looked ill at ease. Sometimes these Calabrians forgot who was in the room when they were talking. They had spent 700 years trying to outsmart the Sicilians, and all of a sudden a Robert de Niro lookalike from Carlton who spoke Italian with an Aussie accent was going to outsmart the Aspanu family. Oh yeah?

The truth was that Guglameno was a pig in a ballgown, a rat with a gold tooth, all razzle dazzle and no dash. If Don Hector found out about this Carlton Calabrian plot, it was goodbye and, grandson or not, Bobby Boy was dead as well. Why couldn't they stick to making money and stop trying to be politicians?

CHAPTER 6

WEDDINGS, SHOOTINGS, ANYTHING

In a dream I saw my screaming death tattooed on the wall.
I awoke and ran to Mexico and heard the devil call
JIMI HENDRIX

For some reason known only to Al Guglameno, Gorgeous George Marcus had been persuaded to return to Sicily with Little Boy Bobby Aspanu and his two silent bodyguards.

Gorgeous George was over the moon at the prospect of meeting the great Don Hector Aspanu, not to mention carrying out yet another secret-agent assignment for his friend and protector Guglameno. George had even invited his latest girlfriend along, a blonde stripper named Jasmyn. When George wanted to butter people up, he knew there was no greater butter than an extra-friendly young lady.

The flight from Melbourne to Rome was not without comedy. The yummy Jasmyn got swept off her feet in first class by a Maltese kickboxer and on landing in Rome was not only a member of the mile-high club several times over but also deeply in love. Gorgeous George was shattered, but he swallowed his pride while Jasmyn swallowed something else. Maltese Dave was in the heavyweight division and George was no fighter. Worse was to come. The meeting with the great Don Hector was a disaster for George.

'Who's this stupid bastardo?' asked Don Hector.

'He's a friend of Guglameno,' said Bobby.

'Oh, I see,' said Don Hector, 'the fuck-up Calabrian sends me a Greek messenger. So, Greek messenger, what the fuck happened to Peter Della Torre, not that I give a shit, but he was a Sicilian.'

'Well,' said George, 'it was all a bit odd. He woke up at three o'clock in the morning to hear a cat meowing.'

'What?' said Don Hector.

'You know,' said George. 'Meow, meow, meow.'

'Yeah, yeah,' said Don Hector. 'Meow, meow. I understand. Then what?'

'Well,' said George. 'Peter gets up and goes outside and he finds a cat in a birdcage in his driveway.'

'A what?' grated Don Hector.

'A cat in a birdcage, grandfather,' said Bobby.

'I heard him,' snapped Don Hector. 'A cat in a birdcage. Then what?'

'Well,' said George, 'he picked the cage up – then, bang,

and Peter's head is lying on the front lawn. Double-barrel shotgun.'

'Jesus,' said Don Hector, puzzled but slightly amused. 'A cat in a birdcage. Couldn't they afford a horse's head? Ha ha.'

'Maybe it was the Albanians,' said Little Boy Bobby.

'Pig's arse,' said Don Hector who, for some bizarre reason talked a bit like Aussie businessman John Elliott with an Italian accent. 'Ya can't blame them for everything. Anyhow, they would eat the bird and fuck the cat. Ha ha ha.' A great one to laugh at his own jokes, the old Don.

'Nah,' he concluded. 'The only people whose tactics defy human logic are the fucking mad Irish. What the hell did Della Torre do to upset those mental cases?'

Everyone looked at each other and shrugged.

'Cats in birdcages,' said Don Hector. 'Jesus Christ! Is the whole world on medication? And what about the fuck-up hit on Joey? I guess you're gonna tell me the fuckin' cat did that as well before he hopped up in the birdcage. And don't blame the fuckin' Albanians for that. Or the stupid Irish. That, my dear grandson, was your fuck-up friends the Calabrians, hey, Bobby?'

It's what you call a loaded question. Loaded with buckshot, and Bobby knew it. As Don Hector spoke, his bodyguards moved in. Benny Benozzo grabbed Little Boy Bobby and swung an ice pick with fearful force with a right-hand blow into the left ear.

Franco Di Tommaso and Luigi Monza froze in horror. As the loyal bodyguards of the suddenly dead Bobby Aspanu, their own lives were in question, but a look from the old man told them to relax. He knew they were only soldiers – and soldiers, however loyal to their capo, owed their final loyalty to the boss, the old general of the clan, Don Hector himself.

Gorgeous George, however, was not so confident or continent just at this moment. He pissed his pants and froze in blind terror as Bobby's body hit the floor.

Don Hector turned to him. 'Tell Guglameno just to make money and not to involve himself in Sicilian family politics. Joey Gravano is my most loyal nephew. Bobby was my most treacherous grandchild. I'm a man with many grandchildren – all Hollywood Sicilian yuppies who try to impersonate Al Pacino. Joey's not too bright, but he is loyal to his uncle and his Godfather.

'My sons and their sons spend all their time counting my money and plotting against me before I'm even in the grave. So, Greek messenger, you go back and tell Guglameno he must thank me for every heartbeat, because he won't ever get a second chance. Now, go home, and let an old man cry for the death of his grandson.'

As George Marcus left, Don Hector spoke in Sicilian to Di Tommaso and Monza. 'Why would that Calabrian send me a Greek messenger?' he spat. 'You know the old Sicilian proverb?'

Di Tommaso replied, 'Never trust a Greek or a priest.'

'Yes,' said Don Hector. 'For Guglameno to trust a Greek we must now ask ourselves about Guglameno. We still have an informer in the camp.

'Who set Della Torre up? And this strange visit from this

nothing Greek on an invitation from Guglameno? Joey killed his own baby brother because we thought he was the informer. Maybe Bobby was the informer. Who knows? But this visit for no reason from this shifty Greek makes me wonder is the Greek the dog? And if he is, then what of his Calabrian master?'

Luigi Monza spoke. 'How do we know the truth, Don Aspanu?'

The old man smiled an evil smile. 'We let it be known that, if the informer isn't found and killed within 30 days, then the relatives of every Calabrian in control in Carlton still living in Italy will all die. Men, women and children.'

Bobby Benozzo spoke. 'That could mean a hundred people, Don Hector.'

'So what?' said the old man. 'A hundred Calabrians mean nothing. If Guglameno is the informer, as Joey secretly thinks he is, then he will kill his Greek messenger and blame him.'

'Then what?' asked Di Tommaso. 'We kill Guglameno?'

'No,' said the Don. 'Once we know the game, we can control the moves. Guglameno can die tomorrow or in ten years' time.'

A funny thing happened. Exactly 30 days after George Marcus flew out of Palermo, he was found shot dead in a quiet street in North Box Hill in Melbourne, outside the address of one of his many girlfriends.

Guglameno had despatched Mario Dellacroce to do the job for $14,000. Dellacroce paid a lot more than that to young Victor Masolino and ordered him to do it. Masolino, having accepted the money, promptly lost his guts and subcontracted the job out to his girlfriend's uncle, an old Aussie gunnie and alcoholic, fallen on hard times. So, for the princely sum of $7000, old Kevin Thackery ended up actually pulling the trigger.

Dellacroce had lost big money to save face. Masolino made money to save face, and poor old Thackery got robbed. As often happens when a job is too hard for the criminal yuppies, they dust the cobwebs of some old Aussie gunman who still thinks a $7000 hit is a good earn.

Guglameno would have used the Albanians for three or four thousand and for that money got a crew of six with a chainsaw, but George had served him well and in keeping with his Hollywood gangster image deserved to die like one. The good thing was, Marcus owed money all over Melbourne and had made serious enemies. His love life was enough to get 20 men shot and it would take the police several years just to question the list of suspects.

As for Guglameno, he would henceforth maintain his secret contacts with the NCA, the DEA and Federal Police through a Jewish lawyer, a lovely lady indeed. And while all this was going on old Poppa Di Inzabella was watching Big Al from a distance with an evil eye, and he let Don Hector Aspanu know that the grave had already been dug for Guglameno. In one year or ten years, it didn't matter. Meanwhile, Guglameno was a money mover at a street level and, as long as he ran his end of things at a profit for all, he lived.

Melbourne, 1994. When a smart Sicilian wants to kill an Albanian in secret, he will hire a Russian, and the Russian will then make a financial arrangement with a Lithuanian. So it was that Vlad Alayla, a Russian marriage broker, money lender and immigration adviser, stood at the bar of the Bavarian Club in West Melbourne with Big Viko Radavic, a half-crazy Lithuanian standover man, talking business of a violent nature.

And so it came to pass that Emma Russell, a 12-year-old schoolgirl, was quietly strolling to school in West Brunswick when she came across the half-dead body of Fracoz Lepetikha. Emma went over to have a look, because she didn't get to see too many dead people as a rule, certainly not on a school day.

She gave the body a little kick and jumped back when Fracoz gave a moan and rolled over on his back. It wasn't a good look. Someone had bashed his face in with a blunt instrument. His top and bottom lips and all his teeth seemed to be missing, one of his eyes had been torn out, and there wasn't much left of his nose. He had holes in his chest as if someone had repeatedly hit him with a hammer.

'Doctor,' groaned Fracoz.

'You OK?' said Emma. 'Ya don't look too good to me, mate.'

'Doctor,' came the voice from the grave, again.

'Do I look like a bloody doctor?' said Emma. She stared at the horrific pulp that was once a face and said, 'You don't come from around these parts, do ya, mate?'

Fracoz tried to raise his arm and got a bloody handprint on Emma's right shoe.

'Get ya fucking hand off me shoe,' she yelped, and gave him a swift kick.

'Ahhhh!' screamed Fracoz.

Young Emma looked around. She was late for school and didn't really have time for this Florence Nightingale stuff. She said, 'My dad told me that if ya nurse a mug he'll die in ya arms. I'm sorry, mate. I'm late for bloody school and ya not dying in my arms.' And with that she marched off to school.

The ghosts of Gravano's mother and sister had returned to claim the life of Fracoz Lepetikha.

Two nights later Joey Gravano sat quietly with Tina in the lounge bar of Squizzy Taylor's Hotel.

Mad Cassandra and her empty birdcage had not reappeared since the night the shots were fired at him and Joey knew that she and her dubious relatives in Collingwood had some role to play in the death of Peter Della Torre. Joey was no genius, but he could conclude that the coincidence was too much to dismiss. But who put the Aussies up to it? Who stood to gain? Then he thought of George Marcus and Guglameno.

'Snap out of it,' said Tina. 'You're day-dreaming.'

Joey came back to life. 'Where's Cassie?' he asked suddenly.

'Oh, she got a job as a table dancer in Tasmania,' said Tina.

'You're joking,' said Joey.

'No,' said Tina. 'She couldn't get out of Melbourne quick enough. She's in Hobart now, works at some dance club in Liverpool Street. She's flashing the map of Tassie down in Tassie.'

Joey laughed, then shook his head and muttered, 'I wonder if she took her birdcage.'

'What do you mean?' asked Tina.

'Private joke,' said Joey. 'Private joke.'

Outside the hotel, Mark Dardo, Niko Ceka and Abdul Kravaritis sat in a 1978 Valiant Regal.

'OK,' said Mark, 'we just give Gravano the best kicking he's ever had.'

'Let's kill him,' said Niko.

'No, no,' said Mark. 'We can't prove he was behind Fracoz getting it.'

'Same fucking dog, different haircut,' said Abdul.

'Like the coppers say,' said Niko, 'if he isn't guilty, then he'll do till we find out who is.'

'No,' said Mark. 'Tonight we just kick the living guts out of the Sicilian snake.'

Niko and Abdul nodded in silence. Mark was the head of the crew and the brains and he had to have a tactical reason for wanting a simple bashing instead of a killing.

They got out of the car and walked to the pub.

Joey Gravano was still sitting at the table with Tina in a world of his own. That's because Tina had her hand under the table, gently caressing his trousers. Joey sat still with his left arm around Tina and a glass of whisky in his right hand. Tina had a gin and tonic in her left hand and a Sicilian trouser snake in her right. The lounge bar was nearly empty.

Something exploded against Joey's head. It felt like a

sledgehammer behind the right ear. He heard Tina scream as blows rained on him. He fell backwards in his chair, and then the kicking started.

He tried to open his eyes but couldn't. He tried to force himself up but the kicking was too heavy and too fast. He felt his top teeth being shattered as a boot crashed into his open mouth. He tried to breathe but choked as a boot hit him in the neck and caught his windpipe. All he could hear was Tina crying and screaming. Then it all faded to black, with the sound of Gene Chandler singing 'Duke of Earl' lingering in his head.

Joey spent three weeks in hospital in a coma. When he recovered he remembered nothing, but when told of the night's events he concluded that to avenge himself on the Albanians would prove only that he was the guilty party behind the murder of Fracoz. Besides, a good bashing now and again is simply the tax all men in any criminal culture pay. It can sometimes be classified under the heading of friendly fire. Anything that involves a nice warm hospital bed afterwards and regular injections of Pethadine once every four hours can hardly be considered serious violence.

Joey was, however, a bit pissed off at having his front top teeth kicked down his neck, but Tina didn't care. To her, Joey was a hero and in the privacy of his hospital room she proceeded to kiss the only part of him the Albanians hadn't kicked in.

When Joey got to the gooey bit he cried out, 'Marry me, baby, marry me!' Tina thought to herself that being offered marriage with her smackers around her loved one's knackers is hardly *Romeo and Juliet*, but she was in love and full of the joys of spring and all. After a moment to regain her composure she said, 'Joey, are you really serious?'

'Yeah,' said Joey. 'Dead-set serious.'

'Ya could have proposed marriage to me after I'd finished, Joe,' she said, pouting a little.

'I'm sorry, Princess. Please, baby, will ya marry me?'

Tina smiled. 'Yeah, Joey, of course. I will, but on one condition.'

'Anything,' said Joey. 'Just name it.'

'Get out of the bricklaying business, Joey. It's too bloody dangerous.'

Joey nodded solemnly. 'I swear on my mother's grave, honey, I'll never lay another brick.' And that, he thought, was one promise he knew he could keep.

The wedding of Joey Gravano and Tina Torre was, at Don Hector Aspanu's insistence, to be held at the Church of the Fisherman on the Palermo waterfront. It was nicknamed the Church of St Juiliano after the great Sicilian hero bandit and legend Salvatore Juiliano.

To get his way, Don Hector claimed ill-health and heart trouble. Most who knew him knew the only heart trouble he had was that he didn't have a heart at all. But, anyway, the Aspanu company paid for Tina's whole family to be flown from Melbourne to Sicily first class and accommodated, all expenses paid. Friends and relations from various corners of the world were ordered to attend, including a gaggle of razzle-dazzle boys from New York, who thought they were tough guys back home but felt like boy scouts at a bum bandits' picnic when they got off the plane in Sicily.

Conversations with the American connections had to be in English as their Italian was hopeless. They had lost any idea of the various Sicilian dialects and Scarchi was a word they had only heard their grandfathers mention in whispers. In true American fashion, they talked loud, splashed plenty of money, produced lavish wedding gifts and offered everyone the benefit of their advice. This was pretty funny, because it led to mob guys talking about junk bonds and computer fraud with Sicilians who were still killing each other over being shortchanged on the sale of a truckload of fish.

For the Americans, it was a step back a hundred years. They were looking at where they had all come from and it secretly frightened and embarrassed them.

They didn't know what to make of strange Sicilian finger signs that had died out everywhere else but were still being used in the old country. The American-Italians were shocked to learn that their much-loved term 'Goombata' – meaning 'my friend' – was also a Scarchi term used by homosexuals when talking about a favourite bum boy. In Sicily, a Goombata was a young friend who was so friendly he would cop it up the clacker. This had some comic results when the Yankee mob guys greeted their Sicilian brothers with 'hey, Goombata'. Guns and knives were drawn and one American wedding guest was shot and two stabbed before Don Hector could call for order and explain the verbal misunderstanding. Most amusing.

Salvatore 'Fat Sally' Gigante wanted to talk with his uncle Hector. Thinking he was some sort of cousin of Joey's, Fat Sally felt Don Hector was his uncle. Don Hector, on the other hand, while politely calling Gigante his nephew, could only recall a Sicilian whore named Gina Gigante that his grandfather and half the village used to screw before they cut her pimp's head off and Gina and her three bastard sons, one of them the sly product of his grandfather, ran away to America.

Fat Sally sat down. They were at a table outside Lorenzo's Cafe on the Palermo waterfront. While the Aspanu clan controlled Sicily with sheer bloodshed, it had little direct influence in America. However, it had life or death influence over the Sicilian crime families, which in turn did have powerful influence with the New York, Los Angeles, San Francisco and Chicago mafia crime families. And it had its own interests all over the world.

In America, Miami was the only city where the Aspanu clan had any direct business. This was because Don Hector had predicted the Cuban trouble in the early 1950s and had made arrangements with contacts in half a dozen South American countries to use Naples as a clearing house to wash cash all through Europe. The Aspanus also controlled heroin and cocaine distribution in France, Spain and Amsterdam and had even backed Afghanistan with money against its various enemies.

'I have a message from our friends in New York,' said Fat Sally.

Don Hector was slightly insulted, but didn't show it. It couldn't be a very important message if they sent a Goombata like this to deliver it, he was thinking. He made a mental note to get Joey to kill this fat faggot when he could find the time. But there was no great hurry.

'What message?' said Don Hector with a thin smile. 'Are our friends in New York so fond of copping dick they no longer want us to export Sicilian salami sausage. Ha ha ha.'

Fat Sally was shocked at this remark but took it as some strange Sicilian comedy, not understanding that the old Don was quite serious.

Franco Di Tommaso and Luigi Monza sat at the next table. They burst out laughing. Bobby and Benny Benozzo were standing six feet away and also joined in the comedy. Sally Gigante thought it polite to also laugh at the old Don's jest.

'So what is your message, Miko mio?'

'My friends want to borrow from you some helpers,' said Sally. 'Little Juilianos.'

'So tell me, little fat boy,' said Don Aspanu, 'what is a bambino Juiliano?'

'A little killer,' said Gigante.

'And, in return for the lend of my bambino Juilianos, I get what?' asked the Don.

Gigante puffed himself up. 'Don Hector Aspanu gets the love, respect and undying friendship of my friends.'

Don Hector nodded then smiled. 'If my name was Marlon Brando, I'd be very pleased but this request indicates you can't trust your own people, so a little money as well as the love, respect and undying friendship would be nice, if your friends don't mind.'

'I will speak to them, Don Hector. How much money?' asked Fat Sally.

Don Hector looked bored. 'Ten per cent of your friends' net operation for as long as they want my friendship.'

Gigante was dumbstruck. This was a fortune.

'I tell you a story,' said Don Hector. 'Many years ago I visit America. I had a friend, a Jew called Meyer Lansky, and another friend, Frank Costello. Lansky, he died of the old age in Miami. Costello, he dead too. But they really give me wonderful time. I fell in love with America, with Hollywood. They introduce me to the only woman I ever loved, a real Hollywood movie-star actress. Her name not important, you too young to remember, anyway. My old friend Frank Costello, some fat former heavyweight dago boxer wanting to climb the ladder took a few shots at Frank, but Frankie lived. The bum who pulled the trigger was named Vincent, Vinnie the Chin, you remember that name, hey?'

Gigante went pale.

'Now,' said Don Hector, 'I hear that the bum who tried to kill my old friend is now a big boss in New York – God only knows how that happened – and he walks around in his dressing gown pretending to be a mad man. Stupido. Tell me, little fat boy, what is his last name?'

Sally choked.

The Don continued calmly. 'Because if the Chin is one of these New York friends, then you can't ask me for help.'

'No,' said Sally, 'he isn't.' He was praying the Don wouldn't request Vincent 'the Chin' Gigante's last name again.

'OK,' said Don Hector, slapping his knee, 'tell your friends we can do the business. But remember, ten per cent or I'll get your friends whacked just for wasting my morning. And their fucking children.'

'Tell me, Don Hector, if I may ask,' said Sally. 'Who was the Hollywood movie actress?'

'Ah,' said Hector, 'just a beautiful woman I lost my head over, then my heart broke and, as fate would have it, she lost her own head. Anyway, young Sally, enough is enough. This is a wedding, a celebration. No more business.'

As Sally walked away, Don Hector said to Di Tommaso in Sicilian, 'Get our friends in Miami to check out our New York friends because they are either fools, desperate or they are trying to play the trick on me. By the way, your English is improving.' He was referring to Di Tommaso's laughter at the dick gag.

'Bobby and Benny are teaching me,' said Di Tommaso.

'Ah,' said the Don with a sharp look at his two bodyguards, 'schoolmasters as well as bodyguards. Hector Aspanu is indeed a fortunate man to have such clever helpers.'

Somehow, they didn't think he meant it.

Italy, 1949. Young Hector Aspanu, Pietro Baldassare and Filippo Della Torre crossed the Strait of Messina from Sicily to the mainland and made their way north to the 'second Sicily', as they called Naples. The Sicilian mafia nicknamed the Naples gangsters 'little brothers' or the 'little cousins' as, next to the gunmen of Sicily, the gangsters of Naples were the only men the Sicilians trusted as men of honour.

Another reason they liked Naples was that the whores there were famous. Prostitution was the backbone of the Naples underworld, but there were plenty of sidelines to go with it. Gambling, blackmail, extortion, robbery, murder, the black market in American cigarettes, whisky or anything else that could be stolen and trafficked. They dealt in drugs to a small degree, as well as medical supplies, weapons, pornography, kidnapping, opium and hashish. They trafficked in teenage boys and girls to the brothels of Morocco, Tunisia, Arabia and North Africa.

But business being as competitive as it is, gangs from Rome and Calabria had moved in and a war had erupted for control of the Naples brothels. Which is why the Naples gangsters called for some young unknown guns to come up from Sicily to help in the battle for Naples.

Those who'd made the call were Carlo Fontana and Danilo Domenico, heads of the La Santa Casa gang. La Santa Casa meant 'the Holy House', and Fontana and Domenico had been Jesuit priests, defrocked and ex-communicated by the Church for crimes the details of which were never revealed. The fact was they were both psychopathic killers whose reputation for violence and sexual excess was legend.

The two former priests turned gang leaders were disappointed that their call for help resulted in three Sicilian gunmen and not 30, but they welcomed Aspanu, Baldassare and Della Torre with open arms.

It was said that the woman who slept in Mussolini's bed, his mistress Clara Petacci, was once a whore from the Naples brothels, and it was her who encouraged Mussolini to execute the bosses of all the Camorra gangs as a payback for the Camorra killing her grandfather and four uncles.

It was also said that, when Mussolini and Petacci were murdered and strung up by the heels in Milan, it was done in Camorra revenge style. Fact or fiction, it all strengthened the legend about the shadowy organisation that controlled the third largest city in Italy, meaning Naples.

To the young guns fresh from the hills of Sicily, Naples was mind blowing. It meant taking money with both hands and an endless supply of women. For the three young Sicilians it was a glittering city of laughter, sex and sin.

It was in reality a filthy, poverty-stricken slum that no self-respecting dog would die in. But compared to the peasant poverty of Sicily it seemed like New York.

It seemed to the Sicilians that they couldn't walk more than ten feet down any narrow street without seeing a whore on her knees or some gangster sticking a knife into the neck of another. The whole city was corrupt and violent. The men robbed and killed. The women whored and robbed and killed. And there was a Camorra war for control of the city. It all needed some Sicilian-style discipline, and so it was that that the three Sicilians sat down with Carlo Fontana and Danilo Domenico in a small brothel and gambling den called the Santa Lucia Club.

'The whole fucking town is bleeding to death in its own vomit,' said Fontana.

'Yes,' said Domenico. 'They kill us, we kill them. Bang,

bang, bang every night but no one wins, no one loses. We rob them, they rob us. We steal their whores, they steal ours. The whole city has become a dog-eat-dog affair.'

Hector Aspanu spoke. 'But I thought the old men of the Camorra controlled the gangs.'

'What old men?' said Fontana. 'The Germans killed the ones Mussolini didn't. Now it's just the young bloods all fighting each other for their own slice of this maggoty pie. You can buy a 12-year-old boy and his 13-year-old sister in the Capri Club for five American dollars each for the whole night and the pimp will, I promise you, turn out to be either the mother or the father. The whole city needs burning in the fires of hell.'

Hector Aspanu spat on the floor. He was trying to follow the conversation but on the other side of the club was the most beautiful girl he had seen, a classic Naples princess. Big seductive eyes, a Roman nose, the full lips of an Arabian harem teaser, a slender neck, black silky hair tied up in a bun and held in place with a Spanish comb. She wore a plain white cotton dress, full and long, tied at her narrow waist with a white belt to reveal a cleavage you could holster a .38 in.

As she walked from table to table selling flowers, her hips swung in time with the music. She was no more than 15, maybe 16 years old. She had a teenage face, but the eyes of a knowing woman years older. She was a girl who had seen things during the war that children shouldn't see.

Men bought flowers from her and she seemed to tolerate

their hands running up under her long white frock to caress the back of her smooth legs. Hector noticed she allowed the American sailors, for a tip, to fondle her firm ripe round arse. But she had rage in her eyes at odds with her smile.

When the girl approached Hector's table, Fontana ordered her away. 'Fucking street rats. I told you before, we don't need fucking flower sellers. Put your arse on the street. You come in here teasing with your flowers, fucking virgin slut. We all know your mother would sell you tomorrow but for your attitude. Get out, whore.'

'I'm not a whore,' spat the young girl.

'Ah, yes,' replied Domenico. 'But you will be, I promise you. Your mother is coming to see me in a week's time. If she hasn't got the money your family borrowed by then, she has promised us that she does have a daughter.'

The young girl started to shake with anger and tears welled up in her eyes. 'My mother wouldn't sell me. You're lying, you pig.'

She ran from the club, crying. At this point Hector Aspanu looked at Baldassare and Della Torre and in Sicilian Scarchi slang said one word. All three men knew that, along with the French dog, the Spanish rat, the Roman pig and the Calabrian snake, these two priests were now also dead men.

Two days later, the head of the French gang leader, Pepe Leon, was found on the steps of the St Januarius Cathedral. The following day the head of the Spanish rats, Torres Garcia, was on the steps. The morning after that the Roman Johnny

Mastrioianni met the same fate, and the day after that the Calabrian Lorenzitti the Gypsy had his head placed on the church steps.

Such public and swift action was a classic mafia trademark, and got a reaction. It was public and violent, quick and simple. Naples went into a state of silent shock and horror. Within days the underbosses and bosses of every street gang in Napoli were calling on the two priests, Carlo Fontana and Danilo Domenico, with gifts of respect. Suddenly the Camorra was coming together, so it would seem, under the leadership of one controlling force, the La Santa Casa gang. However, neither Fontana nor Domenico had seen the three Sicilians since the night of the flower girl.

Then, one night, a small-time Naples gang leader came to visit the priests at the Santa Lucia Club. He was Aniello Sanicola, nicknamed 'The Face' as a result of once having a German rifle butt smashed into his face, making him possibly the ugliest man in Naples.

Fontana and Domenico didn't expect a visit from such a small-time fish, even though he was probably the most frightening and evil little monster in Naples. He simply didn't have the manpower or the guns behind him to claim any true control of anything, but the priests were polite. After all, they were now Dons in their own right. The three Sicilians had seen to that, God bless them.

'I come with the deepest respect, Don Carlo, Don Danilo,' said Sanicola.

They were surprised at being addressed in such a grand and

respectful fashion, and sat back and smiled at the little monster with the horror-movie head.

'No, no,' said Fontana, 'it is we who are honoured that you should call on us. Please sit down.'

'With respect, Don Carlo, I would prefer to stand. I have two messages of some formal importance to give you and it would be rude to deliver such messages while seated.'

The priests sat up.

'Go on, Sanicola,' said Fontana. 'This is most interesting.'

The club was full of whores and Camorra gangsters. The music had stopped and all was very quiet. All ears strained to hear this conversation.

'First of all,' said Sanicola as he reached into his pocket with his left hand and threw down 300 American dollars. 'Here is the money the little flower girl owes you, plus the six months' interest.'

Domenico and Fontana looked at each other in surprise, then back at Sanicola.

'You come here to pay the debt of some whore of a flower girl. Debt paid or not, she belongs to us,' said Domenico.

'I don't think so, Don Danilo,' said Sanicola. 'Little Sophia is under the protection of the Aspanu clan. This message is also from Hector Aspanu.'

The club went deathly quiet. Camorra gunmen in the club who had secretly drawn their weapons in case of a threat to Fontana and Domenico quietly replaced them again. A blind man could see what was coming next, but the two priests were both more than blind, they were arrogant.

'Ha, ha,' Fontana laughed, 'the little Scicoloni slut is under the protection of that Sicilian dwarf Aspanu. What? And we are meant to be afraid? These fucking Sicilians come up here and cut off a few heads and now we are all meant to be afraid.'

Fontana didn't see Sanicola's right hand come out from under his coat. It was holding a 9mm Luger automatic. Fontana didn't hear the shot that killed him but Domenico did, as Fontana fell backwards with a hole in his forehead.

Domenico looked at Sanicola, then dropped to his knees and started to blubber. 'No, no, no, in the name of God, no, no, Holy Mother Mary, please no, Santa Maria, please.'

Sanicola pulled the trigger again and the slug caught the priest in the throat and Domenico gasped and choked and grabbed his neck with both hands, bleeding. As he fell, Hector Aspanu, Pietro Baldassare and Filippo Della Torre walked into the club with Sanicola's gang, all carrying machine guns. Hector was holding the hand of the beautiful flower girl, Sophia Scicoloni.

The next day Hector Aspanu, Pietro Baldassare and Filippo Della Torre sailed out of Naples across the bay. Aniello Sanicola and his gang ruled the Camorra gangs, and Hector Aspanu had left Sanicola with the duty to watch over the health, wealth, wellbeing and future of the flower girl. On his knees before Hector Aspanu, Sanicola swore that only his death would stand in the way of his duty of care.

Sophia Scicoloni, thought Hector as he sailed away. I wonder what will become of her, my little flower girl.

CHAPTER 7

BYE BYE AMERICAN LIE

> *The only two things in life worth a damn are*
> *shooting arseholes and getting your photo taken.*
> MICKY VAN GOGH

Melbourne, 1995. Aussie Joe Gravano sat in the bar of Dan O'Connell's Hotel in Canning Street, Carlton. With him sat Gaetano Lucchese, a young American–Italian, grandson of the old-time New York mafia boss Gaetano Tommy 'Three Fingers Brown' Lucchese.

Young Gaetano liked to be called Little Tommy after his famous grandfather. He was a stockbroker, a law graduate and a screaming faggot, and Aussie Joe was trying hard to keep the conversation away from Little Tommy's urgent desire to get into Joey's pants.

Joey was intending to put Little Tommy and his heroin

investment fund in touch with Simone Tao, thinking that the two should get along like a house on fire as they shared a common interest which involved wrapping their laughing gear around male clients' privates.

Simone had been a little out of sorts with Joey since she hadn't been invited to his wedding in Sicily. However, he had seen her briefly since then and, after allowing her to welcome him in the usual way, for old time's sake, he apologised for not inviting her to the wedding. She accepted but her nose was still out of joint. No wonder, considering where she put it. She was just a bit jealous. The truth was Joey could hardly marry Simone, no matter what she could do between the balance sheets and the bedsheets. Whoever heard of a mixed-race Chinese mafia boss?

Little Tommy, like all Americans, not only felt that he had the wisdom of the ages but also that it was his mission in life to give it to less fortunate people – those unlucky enough not to be Americans.

He was bombarding Joey with tall tales from American criminal history. Joey pretended to listen, but there was only one thing he wanted: a flat million dollars from the ten million Little Tommy had in his company account. Joey wanted to invest five hundred thousand in Australian films and the same in the local music industry.

Little Tommy was in full flight, explaining to Joey his last run-in with the FBI. Then he tapped his nose and said, 'But I can tell you, Joey, I told them shit.'

Unknown to Little Tommy, Simone Tao was on her way to Melbourne from Hong Kong with all the necessary paperwork and documentation for the transfer of funds. Joey had also made arrangements for Tommy Lucchese to be entertained by a giant professional bodybuilder at $2000 a night. Little Tommy had to be kept in Melbourne until he had parted with his funds, legally or by whatever means were necessary. His American mob connections meant shit to the Aspanu clan. However, before anything else, Joey did have one important personal mission to fulfil. Acting on a secret request from Don Hector, he had asked Little Tommy to locate and bring with him a collection of old photographs taken during the late 1940s, 1950s and early 1960s. These pictures had been the property of Jimmy Tarantino, a boxing writer who once ran a gossip magazine called *Hollywood Night Life*.

'You remember to do me that little favour?' asked Joey.

Little Tommy smiled. 'I got it on me,' he said, patting his pocket, and pulled out an envelope and handed it to Joey. 'What's this all about?' he asked. 'I didn't know you were a movie buff.'

'Ah,' said Joey, deadpan. 'Just a favour for a friend.'

'My grandfather and my uncle Willie are in amongst that lot,' said Little Tommy, referring to the photographs. 'There are some very famous faces in that little collection. I hope Don Hector likes them.'

Joey shot Little Tommy a savage glance. 'Who mentioned my uncle's name, you fucking faggot? You mention my uncle's name again and I'll get your dick cut off and I'll feed it to my dog.'

Little Tommy went pale. 'I'm sorry, Joey. Please, it's just that your uncle Hector is in...'

Little Tommy never finished his sentence. He went backwards off the stool he was sitting on and flying across the floor. This minor violence drew little attention from other drinkers in the bar of Dan O'Connell's. A shotgun blast may get a second glance but a bit of a slap hardly caused a ripple.

Little Tommy picked himself up, frightened and embarrassed. Gravano was a fearful, brutal-looking thug of a man. Little Tommy could think of some things he'd like to do with such a big hunk, but being bashed by him wasn't one of them.

'I'm sorry, Joey,' he whimpered.

Joey had put Tommy into the protective custody of Alecoz Samokvic, the bodybuilder who had instructions to attend to him until Simone arrived. Joey went back to the new $2.3 million home in Domain Road, South Yarra, that he had given Tina as a wedding gift. He sat in the flash drawing room, opened the envelope and pulled out a thick pile of old black and white photos.

The very first photo was of Hank Sanicola, Frank Sinatra and Willie Moretti, boss of the old New Jersey family, taken at the Park Avenue Athletic Club. Joey tossed it on the coffee table with hardly a glance.

The second photo was of Frank Sinatra, Marilyn Monroe

and Aniello Dellacroce, underboss of the then Gambino crime family. Interesting, but not what his uncle was looking for.

The third photo was one of Sam Giancana, boss of the Chicago mafia, Angelo De Carlo, Vincent Jimmy 'Blue Eyes' Alo, Johnny Roselli, Frank Sinatra again and Gina Lollabrigida, taken at the Koko Motel in Cocoa Beach, Florida. An interesting snap for anyone who didn't already know of Sinatra's love of being photographed with hoods. Ancient history, common knowledge.

The fourth photo was a heap of mob guys and – believe it or not – John F Kennedy and the peroxide blonde movie star Mamie Van Doren.

Joey put that photo to one side, then pulled out the next one. Mamie Van Doren again and Joey Bonanno, Marilyn Monroe, Aniello Dellacroce and … Hector Aspanu. Joey put that aside as well.

The next was Uncle Hector again with Sam Giancana, Frank Sinatra and John F Kennedy. Next was a porno shot of a naked blonde on all fours with some guy who looked like Sammy Davis Junior in front and another who looked a lot like Dean Martin coming at her from behind. No names or date on the back, but the lady in question looked a lot like Marilyn Monroe.

Then he found the photo he knew his uncle wanted – or one of them. It was of Sam Giancana, J Edgar Hoover and Hector Aspanu himself. Putting it to one side, Joey continued through a collection of movie stars, gangsters, political figures, millionaires, many of them porno photos of the rich and famous. There was one of Rock Hudson doing the business with James Dean. Joey put that aside, too. He knew his uncle put much importance in these photos for one reason: he wanted just one of them very much. The rest, while worth their weight in gold to scandal magazines, meant nothing compared to the one photo he wanted.

There were more porn photos of Marilyn Monroe on her knees with Clark Gable. Another of Marilyn in the same highly compromising position with Montgomery Clift, with Clark Gable in the background with a glass of something in his hand. Rock Hudson again, this time with a large black man chockers. It was all getting a bit boring.

Then he found it. The lost picture of Hector Aspanu and the secret love of his life, the only woman who stole his heart. It was a simple little photo of Hector with Jayne Mansfield, standing in front of Rusar's Jewellery Store in Beverly Hills.

Jayne made Mamie Van Doren and Marilyn Monroe look downright undernourished. She towered over the Don and was built like a blow-up doll.

Toss the rest to the shithouse, the Don had said. But Joey decided to post the one photo to his uncle and keep the rest. Pity he didn't have these back in the 1950s, he thought. All they were now were a pile of magazine photos – worth a lot, but back then they could have got men killed or made others very rich. Joey was holding the winning ticket to the Irish sweepstakes in his hand – 40 years too late.

Three days later, Simone Tao – with the help of Little Tommy Lucchese, a dozen international phone calls, a little computer magic and all the necessary paperwork – had transferred one million into the Gravano Terracotta cement, bricks, slate and paving company of Carlton.

'Not,' said Simone, 'the fanciest name for a million-dollar building and construction company.'

Meanwhile, the other nine million bounced as if by magic from New York to London then to Rome, with half ending up in a Naples account and the other half going into an account held at the Vatican Bank.

Uncle Hector was very pleased when he rang Joey – but wanted to know about the photo.

Joey held the phone to his ear, thinking he had to talk louder because Uncle Hector was not only ringing from Sicily, but also going a little deaf.

He said, 'It's in the post. Yes, Uncle Hector, I posted it. Yes, destroyed all others, I swear. Yes, OK. Yes, yes, Uncle, I'll do that. Yes, yes, I'll take care of it. Yes, I did destroy them. Yes, I'll lose the other thing as well. Yes, I agree. A fucking disgrace, OK?'

And with that Don Hector hung up.

Joey sat and thought. He had just made his uncle nine million dollars richer, and yet all the Don wanted was one photo and a sworn promise that all the other photos were destroyed. And he'd dropped a strong hint that the faggot should go.

Joey was a soldier. He mostly did what he was told. But suddenly he got the idea this pile of old photos was worth more than money could buy. What the hell was in them? He broke his own rule and asked his wife, Tina, who was a movie buff, to have a look at them.

Porno shots and all, there must be a diamond in amongst this lot that only a fool would destroy, and Joey wanted to solve the riddle. He knew he had something important in his hands, but he didn't know what yet.

An hour later, Joey and Tina had the pile of old photos fanned across their big 12-piece dining-room table. Tina was highly excited to be invited to help Joey because since marrying him he had fed her bullshit and kept her in the dark.

She had not forgotten Don Hector's speech at the wedding. 'Woman are like a deck of cards: Ya need a heart to love 'em, a diamond to keep 'em, a club to belt 'em with and a spade to bury 'em. In my experience, ladies and gentlemen, all women work by the inch, want by the yard and should be kicked by the foot.'

Don Hector's speech was regarded as most comic and greeted with much laughter, but Tina suspected the old man was deadly serious. This was the first time her husband had allowed her to take part in something she knew was family business. She was eager to help and flattered to be asked.

'You know all about Hollywood movie history, don't ya, bubby?' said Joey. 'Marilyn Monroe and all that shit?'

'Yeah,' said Tina. 'I've read everything ever written on Marilyn Monroe, Frank Sinatra, the Kennedy clan, all that movie mobster political gossip crap. It's fascinating.'

'Well,' said Joey, 'cast your eye over this lot. I reckon it's an historical photo collection worth a fortune, but Uncle Hector told me to destroy them all except for one of him and Jayne Mansfield.'

'Shit,' said Tina. 'Uncle Hector knew Jayne Mansfield?'

'Evidently pretty well,' replied Joey.

Tina glanced over the collection. 'Oh look,' she said. 'He's much younger here, but wasn't he at our wedding? And look who he's standing next to.'

She was pointing at an old shot of a much younger Don Pietro Baldassare holding hands with a wild-eyed brunette with a big mouth and a fixed smile.

'That's Don Pietro,' said Joey. 'Who's the mad-eyed moll next to him?'

'That,' said Tina, 'if I'm not mistaken, is Jacqueline fucking Kennedy.'

Joey looked at the back of the photo and read the scribbled writing. 'Ciro's Nightclub, Hollywood,' it read. But no names, no dates.

'Joey,' said Tina quietly, 'I think that is a very important photo.'

He nodded. Tina went through others. John F Kennedy with various movie stars and mobsters. Then she came across a photo of JFK and Jackie Kennedy with Pietro Baldassare. Then a photo of JFK, Marilyn Monroe and, again, Pietro Baldassare. Then another photo of Baldassare with Johnny Roselli, Sam Giancana and Jackie Kennedy.

'Jesus,' said Joey, 'I missed these ones.'

'Shit,' said Tina, 'a photo of fucking Fidel Castro.'

Joey grabbed it. Sure enough, it was a photo of Castro, Jayne

Mansfield and Meyer Lansky. But that was impossible, thought Joey. Everyone in the world knew of the mad CIA White House mafia plot to kill Castro – yet here was a photo of the Jewish financial genius behind the whole American mafia and the only actress in America that Fidel Castro publicly said was built like a real woman. If the mob really had been planning to hit Castro, this photo proved they weren't trying too hard. Unless they'd hired Jayne Mansfield to screw him to death.

Don Hector always told him, 'When buttering up an enemy or a friend use butter that spreads easy,' and Miss Mansfield was without a shadow of a doubt the most famous leg spreader in Hollywood. So, who knows, maybe this photo proved the plot happened.

Then Tina squealed. 'I don't believe it! Are these photos real? No, it can't be.'

She had a photo of three men and a blonde taken at the Waldorf Astoria Hotel in New York.

'This is it, Joey, this is it. I don't bloody well believe this.'

Joey looked at the photo. It was Don Pietro Baldassare, Johnny Roselli, some nobody Joey didn't recognise and Marilyn Monroe.

'Yeah,' said Joey. 'So what, Poppa Pietro went to America in the 1950s with Uncle Hector and met a lot of people.'

'Joey, Joey, Joey,' said Tina. 'Look at the guy sitting next to Marilyn Monroe.'

Joey looked and shook his head. 'He don't look like no one to me.'

Tina couldn't believe Joey didn't recognise the face. 'Joey,' she said patiently, 'either these photos are all fakes or that is a photo of Marilyn Monroe cuddling Lee Harvey Oswald.'

Joey gave Tina a blank look.

'The guy who shot President Kennedy in Dallas, Texas,' Tina hissed, rolling her eyes.

He suddenly came to life. 'Oh, yeah. I remember. I was about eight or nine years old when that happened, but everyone reckoned the CIA or the commies or the mafia did it, anyone but Oswald. He was supposed to be just the mug who copped the blame, the patsy.'

Tina couldn't get her words out quick enough. 'He was also meant to be a lone wolf, no friends, knew no one, a nut, a commie crackpot – so what's he doing with fucking Marilyn Monroe all over him like a rash? Poppa Pietro is with Johnny Roselli – wasn't he the whacker trying to kid everyone the government had hired him or Sam Giancana or Santo Trafficante to kill Fidel Castro? I read a book on it someplace,' said Tina.

This was all a bit much for Joey. 'I don't get it,' he said. 'Who gives a shit if Oswald did know Marilyn Monroe?'

Then Joey remembered Uncle Hector's butter-up theory. He thought about Poppa Pietro, Jacqueline Kennedy, Lee Harvey Oswald and Marilyn Monroe being pictured together. All this at the same time the mafia were kidding the CIA. They were putting together a hit on Fidel Castro then, bang, Kennedy gets it in the head and then Oswald gets it from a mafia puppet, Jack Ruby.

'So,' said Joey, 'what do these photos prove, Tina?'

'They prove,' she said slowly, 'that people who pretend they didn't know each other really did. They don't really prove anything more, but they suggest a great deal. I don't know anything, but, from a woman's point of view, Joey, if I found out you were fucking Marilyn Monroe behind my back, I'd kill you.'

'But Kennedy dumped Monroe.'

'So,' said Tina, 'instead of one woman who wanted him dead you have two. Jacqueline Kennedy had the money, Marilyn Monroe had the pussy. Between the two of them, they knew everyone worth knowing, from the devil to the Pope.'

'What are you saying, Tina?' asked Joey, not quite getting it.

'Well, it's just my opinion, but after seeing these I reckon Oswald did pull the trigger, but that Kennedy's wife put the whole thing together, the mafia oversaw operations, at the same time kidding the CIA and the White House they were going to whack Castro. And Marilyn Monroe, either knowingly or unknowingly, was used as the psychological sweetener.'

She warmed to her theory. 'It's obvious, Joey. Jacqueline Kennedy set her own husband up for it. I mean, he did give her VD and he gave Monroe a nice dose as well. Jesus, Joey, if you gave me VD, I'd cut ya fucking heart out with a butcher's knife while you slept.'

Joey was aghast. 'So all this shit, all these photos sort of prove or suggest that Kennedy's wife set him up for a hit using his own mistress to butter up the hitman, and the mob not oversaw operations and killed the hitman afterwards, all nice and tidy?'

'Yes,' said Tina. 'That's about it.'

'Well, big deal. It's the fucking 1990s, for Christ's sake. Who gives a flying shit?'

'Well,' said Tina slyly, 'if your uncle wants these photos destroyed so badly, then someone important obviously does give a shit.'

She had a point. Even Joey could see that.

Little Tommy Lucchese never made it to the airport for his flight home. He was lying in the OK Motel in North Carlton with a bullethole in the back of his skull. Next to him lay the bodybuilder with three shots in the back and one in the head. Little Tommy had been mutilated. Someone had cut his dick off.

Police investigated it as a homosexual murder and questioned almost all Melbourne's homosexual and criminally related homosexual community. Had they questioned Aussie Joe Gravano's pit-bull terrier they may have got a tidbit of information, as Pugsley had eaten the missing tidbit in question.

Photos of Pugsley eating were sent to Sicily and America as the wish to have Little Tommy clipped had come from Bobby Boy Alderisio in New York.

'Ah, well,' Don Hector had said, 'morals and money. Without one, you'll starve to death. Without the other, you'll lose your soul, and we lost our soul a long time ago. God only has us on Sundays. The rest of the week we're at the Devil's table.'

Joey sat and wondered at the lie and the false pretence of it all. He was part of a system supposedly held together by a common background of nationality, culture, tradition and an alleged code of honour. The truth was, it was held together by an international body of men – some of them saints, most of them snakes, all with the same common interest – wealth, power and the continued survival of this thing they called La Cosa Nostra Soldati.

Joey laughed to himself. It beat being a fucking bricklayer.

CHAPTER 8

A BAD JEW WITH A .22

Melbourne, 1996. Matchstick Marven Mendelsohn was a long, lanky, baby-faced, blue-eyed smiling mental case who worked for himself as the Melbourne crime world's version of a subcontractor. Marven smiled at everyone but owed loyalty to no one except his dear old mother, who washed his shirts and underpants for him.

Professional killers who live with their mothers are generally a precious lot, and Marven was no different. He had his quaint little ways. For example, he would never shoot anyone on Saturday as on Saturday he took his mother to the synagogue.

Marven was, as far as his mother Esther was concerned, the very model of a good Jewish boy. The nickname 'Matchstick' came about as the result of an unfortunate mishap involving

Marven's tying a gentleman to a chair in a garage in Cruikshank Street, Port Melbourne, dousing him with petrol and setting him alight.

Marven only ever did it the once and ever since avoided fire and the use of fire in his work. He was known to bitterly resent the fact that one small to medium mishap with a match should earn him not only a childish nickname but a rather unsavoury reputation as some sort of nutty fire bug. A more accurate nickname would be Magic Marven. This is because Marven had the knack of making people vanish into thin air.

Marven's one true love, next to his dear mother, was his car. It was his pride and joy, a 954 Studebaker Landcruiser 232 V8 automatic, in gleaming white mint condition. He had it imported from America and at some considerable cost had it changed from left-hand to right-hand drive. Marven had spent more money on the old car than it was worth but, of course, price is no object when love is involved. Marven's late father had died at the wheel of a 1954 Studebaker Landcruiser and it was the only car his dear mother felt comfy in. Mind you, his mother was not fond of her late husband because she had once discovered him in bed with the cleaning lady, a rather seductive Filipino girl.

To add insult to injury, when Mrs Mendelsohn had come home early one day to discover her husband banging away, he had simply made a temporary withdrawal, walked over and closed the bedroom door in his good lady wife's face, then left her standing in the hallway in tears listening to the cleaning girl moan as her husband finished the job.

Needless to say, Mrs Mendelsohn had been shocked, hurt, ashamed and deeply jealous. She cried so much she could hardly see as she cut the brake cable of her husband's much loved Studebaker. After his death in a most unfortunate road accident shortly afterwards, she was determined to get another Studebaker. Husbands come and go, but a 1954 Studebaker is forever.

She was a careful woman, and sacrificing a lovely car to rid herself of an unfaithful husband filled her with mixed emotions: joy at getting away with it, sadness that the car had to be destroyed in the process. So, when young Marven replaced the family car all was well in the Mendelsohn household. Except, of course, for the cleaning lady, who was promptly replaced with a little old Greek woman. The only moaning she did was when she received her weekly pay packet.

Anyway, one day Marven parked the old Studebaker in the car park at Tullamarine Airport. An important overseas visitor from Italy was arriving, a very old and much-loved and respected gentleman called Don Pietro Baldassare. He was being met at the airport by a host of assorted relations, friends, Sicilians and countrymen.

Lend me your tears, thought Marven with a smile. It was broad daylight, in front of a hundred or more people. The joint was full of police, security cameras, and onlookers. It was the toughest task in the most impossible place and so given to the one Jew in Melbourne insane enough to attempt the impossible, and with the cheek to get away with it.

Marven didn't like working for the dagos even though he

had in the past. He preferred to work for Aussies. This was an Aussie-ordered hit, with five men all tossing $10,000 each into the pot, cash in Marven's hand before the job. To Marven, why the hit had been ordered was not important. How to do it and how to get away with it, that was the only concern.

Marven entered the airport wearing a bright floral silk shirt, suggesting to anyone who saw it that the wearer had recently returned from Surfers Paradise. The big blue eyes were covered with sunglasses and his number-three crewcut gave Marven a schoolboy look.

Under his flowing floral shirt he had a cute Smith and Wesson .22-calibre revolver fitted with a specially designed Colt Walker silencer. The ammo was short sub-sonic soft-nosed hollow point.

The old Don was in his late seventies by all accounts, dying of lung cancer and on a world trip before he kicked the bucket. Marven wanted to make sure he died of lead poisoning first – which, of course, would be a more merciful end. Marven knew he couldn't get the old gentleman with a clean head shot, as that would mean pulling the gun out and raising his arm to head level in front of a hundred people. So, on the best medical advice, Marven was planning something else. He'd been told that an elderly gent with cancer would not survive several bulletholes in the stomach. He might get to hospital, but he'd die.

Marven was also a bit of a psychologist. He knew that people run from a fallen dead man but rush to help a wounded one, and in the panic Marven planned to get away unnoticed. The idea was simply to let the old dago get through Customs, then clip him 30 feet from the main exit doorway or as he was coming down the escalator. Which was easier said than done.

Joey Gravano, Tina and a small army of Sicilian and other assorted Italian types greeted the old Don with a show of great emotion.

Customs was quick and, after a short while, with all bags gathered, the old man and his horde of excited friends and relatives made their way towards the main exit. Outside was a line of six 1988 Lincoln town car stretch limos. No expense was spared for Don Pietro's arrival. He was to stay as a personal guest of Joey Gravano at his home in Domain Road, South Yarra.

As the old man approached the main door, he suddenly looked down at his stomach – not so much in pain as in disbelief. He put his hand up to his stomach as another small hole appeared in his shirt. Then blood appeared, and another puncture hole appeared in his white shirt. For a moment people close to him thought the cancer in him had burst his stomach. Then two more small holes appeared in his shirt, making five. Gravano realised at once that the old man had been shot and looked around frantically for the offending party. He turned back to see Don Pietro drop to his knees.

'Ahhhh,' he moaned. He pitched face forward, but was caught by people around him.

No one saw Marven standing by the hire-car counter with the cute little pistol in his left hand under his flowing shirt. People milled around, thinking the elderly gentleman was having some sort of collapse or heart attack. Marven quietly walked out.

Two police rushed past him to see to the emergency as he drove away. He picked up his car phone and rang the Big Bad Blonde Agency and ordered up a lady, as was his habit after a bit of excitement. He liked to relax and he had a regular lady. His mother would be outraged if she knew, because she was a German girl built like a Nazi beauty queen. But it all appealed to Marven's twisted sense of humour. Killing an Italian, then fucking a German, he giggled to himself. A few Jews in Melbourne would be able to see the comic side of that. Ha ha.

He had other thoughts as he drove along. He wondered if Jewish hitmen were getting smarter or Italian gangsters were getting dumber, as it seemed the easiest 50 grand he had ever earned. An airport full of people and no one jerried. Dress like a clown and people think you are one. Never do a hit dressed like a nightclub gangster.

A week after the death of the old dago Don, in a nightclub called The Men's Gallery in Liverpool Street, Hobart, a long-legged table-dancer with a cheeky smile and laughing eyes was busy swinging her vanilla-ice-cream arse about the place, to the thunderous applause of male onlookers. There were various other Penthouse Pet-type yummies swinging themselves about as well. The audience was showing enormous interest. One old gentleman, in particular, seemed on the point of a heart attack because of the undivided attention he was getting from Cassandra Connor. Her bum was about an inch from the old bloke's nose when she looked up to see three old faces she hadn't seen in a long time. They belonged to Micky Kelly, Mad Benny Shapiro and Matchstick Marven Mendelsohn. Cassie squealed with delight and ran into the open arms of Micky Kelly and started kissing his face and neck like a happy puppy who's been promised a big bone.

Wiggling and giggling, she gushed, 'When did you get out, Micky? I didn't know you was out.'

Micky freed himself from Cassie's grasp and she then grabbed Mad Benny and Marven at the same time.

'Calm down, kid,' said Micky.

But Cassie couldn't relax. 'God, it's good to see some old faces for a change,' she said.

Micky smiled. 'When I told you to piss off out of Melbourne for a while, I didn't expect you to come this far south,' he said.

Cassie was wearing nothing but a high-cut thong bikini bottom that left little to the imagination, a pair of stiletto heels, and a garter belt around the top of her right leg stuffed with money. Her bikini bottom was also holding a fair amount of paper money that had been placed there by sweaty hands.

Mad Benny patted Cassie on the arse and said, 'Doin' OK, then, Cassie?'

'Listen, Benny,' she said, 'a fat lady with a wooden leg would make money down here. American sailors, merchant seaman, Japanese fishing boats. It's money for jam, I'm tellin' ya.'

The following morning Cassie woke up in a queen-size bed in a plush suite of rooms in the Wrest Point Casino. Beside her lay Micky Kelly, still asleep. The fog started to roll away from her hungover brain.

Micky had wanted her all night long so he'd played roulette downstairs while Cassie took Mad Benny and Mental Marven (she'd always called the lone-wolf killer 'Mental' and was the only girl allowed to get away with such familiarity) upstairs with the intent of polishing them off quick smart. After all, it was Micky who had just got out of prison and so, according to the Robbers Rule Book, Page 47, sub-section 3, was fully deserving of any and all available snatch on offer.

Cassie slowly moved out of bed and made her way to the bathroom. As she passed a side table she saw a pile of $100 bills big enough to choke a mule. She stopped to look. They were folded into bundles of what she guessed were 50 notes apiece. That made five grand a bundle, and she counted 12 bundles of hundreds. She dimly remembered Micky saying something about roulette.

She decided Micky couldn't have won that much at roulette. She made her way into the bathroom, got under the shower and began to lather up.

She could be a bit naughty now and then, but only for the

right bloke – or blokes, as the case may be – and they were few and far between. But she had to admit to herself that, when the right blokes did show up, she tended to lose the plot a bit in the sexual morals department.

Just as she was considering the pros and cons of all this in a lather of soap suds, steam, hot water and daydreams, Micky Kelly pulled the shower screen back.

'Hey, Cassie,' he said. 'How would you like to pretend to be a lawyer and go in to Risdon Prison and visit Hacker Harris for us?'

Cassie looked at Micky as if he was mad.

'Don't worry, Princess, I got all the badge identification for ya.'

'Hacker Harris,' said Cassie. 'They kicked him out of the Collingwood Crew on the grounds of mental illness. He needs a psychologist, not a fucking lawyer.'

'Now, now, now,' said Micky, trying not to laugh. 'Don't be sarcastic.'

He shut the shower screen to let Cassie finish her shower in peace.

Sarcastic, thought Cassie, how can you make a sarcastic remark about an old gunnie who thinks he is the reincarnation of Garry fucking Cooper?

The following day, Cassie arrived at Risdon Prison, otherwise known as the Pink Palace, in a hire car, a well-cut suit, bare legs and high heels. The black skirt was cut tight around the hips and showing enough leg to put a smile on the screws' faces. She was directed to the medium-security unit at the side of the jail.

Prison security was so lax they didn't even ask her to produce any identification. Evidently a big smile and a good set of legs was all that was needed. She gave them her name and said she was a lawyer and would like to see Hacker Harris. Five minutes later she was sitting in the contact visit area with the old cowboy from Collingwood. And, true to form, after passing on the message from Micky Kelly and getting the information Micky needed, she naturally thought Hacker would urgently request a Monica Lewinsky. Cassie had been sent into visit guys in prison before, and she knew she could hardly say no to a presidential request for a spot of executive relief.

But all Hacker wanted to know was if Cassie could help him with the correct words to the *Beverly Hillbillies* song. So she sat there, all legs and big eyes, in total disbelief at this insane request as she sang the song to a delighted Hacker Harris.

Hacker laughed his head off and waved Cassie goodbye as he walked away singing the old song to himself.

When Cassie got back to the casino Micky Kelly asked, 'Did he tell ya?'

'Yeah,' she said, still not really believing what she'd just done. 'He said it's buried in the back of a house in Thomas Street, Yarraville. Albanian Billy's place.'

'Jesus,' said Micky, 'Bronco bloody Billy's joint.'

Even the two Jews looked a little worried at this news.

'What is it?' asked Cassie.

Micky explained. 'Hacker Harris is the only crook in Australia who owns two 84mm Carl Gustov anti-tank guns, nicknamed the Charlie Gutsache.'

'Yeah,' said Benny, 'and six boxes of M26 hand grenades, as well as bloody jumping-jack landmines.'

'Yeah, well,' said Marven, 'ya can't bag a bloke for taking precautions.'

'Jesus Christ,' said Micky. 'Precautions! The mad bastard's got more guns than God – or he did have. He gave the Collingwood crew all his small arms before he moved to Tassie. But what possessed him to give the military gear to the fucking Albanians? M79 grenade launchers, landmines, hand grenades. Ya know he had the largest privately owned collection of handguns of any crim in Australia at one stage, not to mention all the military stuff. Bloody flamethrowers, the lot.

'Luckily he was only a mad collector and only ever used a handgun, but the fact that he had this gear kept a lot of people in line for a long time, and now you're telling me Bronco fucking Billy has got the anti-tank guns. Jesus, Cassie, you have to go and see Hacker again and get him to ring Billy for us.'

'Do I have to?' said Cassie.

'Ah come on,' said Benny, 'what's the poor bloke want in return? A blowie? Big deal.'

Cassie sighed. 'That, I can deal with. But I don't know that I want to sit through another hour of the *Beverley Hillbillies*.'

The boys looked puzzled.

'Don't worry about it,' said Cassie, 'if I told ya, you wouldn't believe me.'

Next night Micky, Benny, Marven and Cassie were enjoying fine Italian cuisine at the Prego Restaurant in Macquarie Street, Hobart.

'Well,' said Micky, 'you've done well, Cassie.'

'Yeah,' said Cassie. 'Old Hacker will ring Bronco Billy and tell him to expect you.'

'That's a relief,' replied Benny. 'I don't fancy knocking on Bronco's door saying, "Excuse me, but may we borrow one of your two anti-tank guns, please."'

Marven laughed. 'Albanians placed in charge of military hardware – it's a frightening thought.'

Micky Kelly thought for a moment about his own rather close relationship with the Albanian mafia via Mark Dardo and his clan. Bronco Billy came from another Albanian criminal clan and that clan owed their loyalty to Hacker, so good manners must be strictly adhered to, otherwise both Albanian clans could take offence. Good manners was the name of the game in the arms and ammo area, especially when dealing with rival Albanian clans.

Micky knew that the trip to Tassie had been worth it. The Aussie crews and the Albanians had a friendship he couldn't afford to shatter because of some stupid breach of protocol.

'No, Cassie,' said Micky, 'you've done bloody well.'

'By the way,' said Cassie, 'Hacker wanted to know if you knew how to load an 84mm Carl Gustov anti-tank gun?'

Micky stopped eating. 'Well, no, not really, but there shouldn't be much to it.'

Cassie continued. 'Hacker reckons the ammo's a bit funny looking.'

'How do ya mean?' asked Micky.

'Well,' said Cassie, 'it's shaped a bit like a heavy tube with a sort of spiky point sticking out of one end.'

'Excuse me,' said Benny, 'and correct me if I'm wrong, but Hacker did tell you how to operate an 84mm anti-tank gun, didn't he, Cass?'

'Yeah,' said Cassie, 'but it sort of didn't make sense.'

'Ah, don't worry,' said Micky, 'Marven will figure it out, won't ya, Marv?'

The blue-eyed Jew smiled and nodded, but secretly hoped he could nut it out, as he had never even seen an anti-tank gun, let alone loaded or fired one.

'Yeah,' said Micky, 'a gun's a bloody gun. There can't be much to it, can there?'

All agreed and continued eating and polishing off their wine.

Next day, it was time for Micky and the Jews to leave. A few morning drinks at the Alabama Hotel in Liverpool Street followed by a light lunch, then it was off to the airport for more drinkies and a tearful goodbye from Cassie.

'Try to pop in to see old Hacker now and again, Cassie,' said Micky.

'Ya know,' interjected Benny, 'Tassie's not a bad place really.

At least a bloke can come down here and win a game of spot-the-Aussie, and the cops seem pretty laidback.'

'Yeah,' replied Cassie, 'they are pretty easy-going. Every now and again they take a turn for the worse and stick a gun in some poor bugger's backyard, but, all in all, they try not to shoot ya at the drop of a hat.'

The boys all nodded in agreement. The police shootings in Melbourne had reached almost comic heights.

'The only problem down here,' Cassie went on, 'is the silly buggers are sitting on a goldmine and don't know it. They are so busy looking at the bloody trees they can't see the wood. They have a Bible in one hand and a photo of Queen Victoria in the other and refuse to budge an inch. You'd think that with two bloody heads they'd be twice as bloody smart, but they're not.'

Micky nodded. 'One thing's for sure, Cassie. With weather like this there's no chance of a Vietnamese takeover.'

'Yeah,' said Benny, laughing. 'The Viets don't like the snow. Ha ha.'

'Don't be too bloody sure,' said Marven. 'There's nothing stopping the little scallywags from buying warm coats.'

When the boys got on the plane Micky looked back at the last state in Australia that could be called a true-blue Aussie stronghold and wondered if Cassie was right — or if the world would jump up one day and bite poor old Tassie in the arse.

As the plane took off, Micky shook his head. The sun set on the empire a long long time ago, he thought. One day these poor simple-hearted, true-blue bastards are gonna wake up in fright and, like the rest of Aussie land, realise that Banjo Paterson is dead and the land of Oz belongs to fuckin' Uncle Sam and the Japs.

Ah well, thought Micky, as long as the Aussie crews have got all the guns, we'll never be beaten, not by other crims, at any rate. The rest of Australia might like it up the arse from the Yanks and the Japs but in the criminal world ground is too hard to win just to simply surrender it. As far as Micky was concerned, Banjo Paterson was still alive and well ... but now he carried a loaded gun. Ha ha.

CHAPTER 9

JAYNE MANSFIELD AND THE MAFIA DON

I've always been a sucker for a good-lookin' guy.
JAYNE MANSFIELD

Punta Raisi Airport, Sicily, 1996. On the tarmac was a Boeing. In the cargo hold was a coffin. In the coffin was what was left of Don Pietro Baldassare after the Australian pathologists had opened him up with a Black & Decker to count how many bullets were in him and check out how much damage they'd done. The answer was five bullets and plenty of damage. The old bastard had been dead on arrival at hospital after the little welcome to Melbourne so neatly arranged by Matchstick Marven and his toy .22.

Aussie Joe Gravano had flown across to escort the coffin home to the old country, the least he could do in the circumstances. Don Hector Aspanu met him. The old Don looked on stonily as his bodyguards took charge of the coffin.

'Jesus!' yelled Don Hector when the boys nearly dropped the coffin. 'Take it easy.'

As Don Hector watched the body of his old friend being loaded into the back of the 1959 Cadillac hearse, he said to Joey, 'There goes the man who disposed of the body of fucking Jimmy Hoffa, the great American mystery. And he gets whacked at the airport in fucking skippy nut nut land, fucking Australia.'

Joey was shocked. 'Don Pietro got rid of Jimmy Hoffa?'

'Yeah,' said Don Hector, 'chrome-coating chemical vat in Detroit, 1975. I ordered the hit. Pietro went over to see it and make sure it went to plan.'

'Jimmy Hoffa,' said Joey, impressed. 'The big boss of the American Teamsters Union.'

The old Don nodded. 'Yes, life is a funny thing, Joey. All the boys go to meet fucking Hoffa in Bloomfield, Detroit, 30 July 1975, at the Machus Red Fox Restaurant. He owed us a fucking lot of money.'

'So why kill him?' asked Joey.

'Coz he no fuckin' pay,' said the Don. 'Anyway, we never had to fucking kill him. The fat pig had the fucking heart attack at the fucking restaurant. Pietro tell me. He eat noodles, macaroni, spaghetti, pizza, then fucking two plates linguine, then he have fucking sugar-coated fried pastry and two bottles of imported grappa. He fucking burp, drop dead. No wonder.

'Well, Pietro couldn't believe it, so the boys melt the body in the chemical factory and the big "Who killed Jimmy Hoffa Mystery" begins. And this just like that,' he added.

'How do you mean, Uncle?' asked Joey, puzzled.

Don Hector almost laughed.

Joey was almost laughing at the Hoffa story while trying to maintain a sombre look. The truth behind most underworld mysteries was either very simple or very stupid. It wasn't so much organised crime as disorganised comedy at times. Jimmy Hoffa – who would ever in a million years believe he killed himself on an overdose of linguine?

'Don Hector,' said Joey, 'where they gonna bury Don Pietro?'

'Catania,' said Hector. 'We gotta drive to Catania first, then over to that shithole Castellammare del Golfo.'

'Jesus,' said Joey. 'Castellammare del Golfo, that's 50 fucking miles away. Little America.'

'Yeah,' said the Don, 'but we gotta be polite.'

The seaside town with the long name had the reputation, along with towns like Cinisi and Corleone, as mafia strongholds. The truth was that American-Italian gangsters from Milan, Rome, Calabria, and Naples returned to Italy during the 1920s and 30s and bought holiday villas in such places, thus reinforcing the great American myth about them.

The Don didn't care. His old friend Pietro Baldassare was a true Sicilian, and if his bastard grandchildren in Castellammare del Golfo wanted to cry and kiss Don Hector's ring, well, it would be rude not to let them.

It was a long drive to Castellammare del Golfo. Joey pulled

the old car up in front of a particular cafe on the waterfront, and he and the old Don went inside. They were greeted by a small gathering of men. This included Dominic Scarvaci, a killer who had just been released from prison in Rome, and Tommy Greco, a heavy heroin trafficker who represented one of the major New York crime families, the Bonanno clan.

Many lesser lights were there, waiting for Don Hector to give his blessing for Tommy Greco to take over the Baldassare clan. Don Hector wasted no time. He kissed Tommy warmly on both cheeks, then on both Tommy's eyes and his forehead. Only an old Scarchi Sicilian sitting in the corner of the cafe understood, and smiled. Tommy Greco had just received a kiss on each cheek for welcome, one on each eye for blessing – and one on the forehead for goodbye. Tommy didn't know it, but he was a dead man.

As the old Sicilian proverb goes, 'Anything bought can be sold but what you kill for, you keep.' The point was, Tommy Greco had bought his way into power, and so had no real grip on it. Under Sicilian rules, you just don't buy votes like some politician. The mafia there was a military dictatorship, not some Yankee pork barrel democracy.

The Don sat down and a drink was brought to him. Strong grappa, like liquid fire. A picture on the wall caught his eye. It was a very old Playboy Playmate of the month centrefold of Miss Jayne Mansfield. Miss February, 1955. Her measurements were printed underneath: 40, 21, 35.

'Ah, Jesus Christ,' said Hector Aspanu softly. 'Holy Mother of God, she was a woman.'

'You knew her?' asked Tommy Greco.

Don Hector nodded. 'Yes, I knew her.'

He sat back and finished the grappa. As another was poured for him, Tommy Greco lit the long thin cigar the Don had put to his lips. Hector took a deep draw on the cigar and blew out the smoke and the gathered men waited in silence for a story they hoped would follow. They got it.

'Baldassare and me, we go to America regular in the 1950s to see all the boys,' the Don began. He listed a Who's Who of American mobsters of the era, the heads of every heavy crime family in the States.

'You were going to tell us about Jayne Mansfield, Don Hector,' Tommy Greco reminded him.

'Ah yes,' said the old Don with a smile. 'In 1955 Frank Sinatra, Sam Giancana, Baldassare and me were having drinks at the Union Club, Hoboken. Then Trafficante and Profaci joined us with Vito Genovese, so we go to see the boxing at Madison Square Garden on Fifteenth Street and Eighth Avenue, New York. This was a Friday night. After the fight we go to all the big clubs. It was a big night. Sinatra asked me if I wanted lady. I say who. He says he can get me either Marilyn Monroe or Mamie Van Doren, and they got the tits like the ripe grapefruit. I tell him in Sicily we don't like the grapefruit, we like the big watermelon. Ha ha. I was the guest of George Boomer, owner of the Waldorf Astoria Hotel, New York. Next morning about 11am I wake up to knock on door and there was Jayne Mansfield. Oh my God, all my dreams come true. I fall in love like the fuckin' thunderbolt.'

Joey Gravano smiled slyly to himself at the way his uncle Hector was talking. He'd noticed that, when his uncle was in the company of American Italians visiting Sicily, he spoke in broken English, playing the humble old Sicilian peasant role. The truth was Hector Aspanu was a very polished and educated old gentleman who spoke several tongues and had been speaking English longer than most of the men gathered had been alive.

'She was fucking beautiful,' continued Don Hector.

'Ahh yes, Vera Jayne, that her real name. Vera Jayne Palmer. She married some bum named Paul Mansfield so she pinched his name. She just finished movie called *Hell On Frisco Bay*, and the boys put in money for another movie for her.

'Fucking Sinatra tell her I can help her in the movies. Jayne a good girl and very smart, she have da fucking IQ of 163, very bright girl. Anyway, I invite her in to my room. She no mess about. "My name Jayne Mansfield, Mr Aspanu," she says, and we shake hands. "Mr Aspanu," she say, "Mamie Van Doren told me that for a girl to get any place in Hollywood she had to learn to swallow her pride along with as many movie producers as she can get her mouth around. I'm told you like the watermelons and not the grapefruit. Ha ha."

'Then she giggle and wiggle and smile and with a flick of two little buttons the top of her dress come undone and, holy mamma mia, out pop the biggest set of tits I ever see. I stood there with my fucking mouth open. She not a very shy girl. Then she just get down on her knees right in the hotel-room hallway and undo my pants.

'"Mr Aspanu," she said, looking up to me. "There's a movie coming up called *Girl Can't Help It*. They want Mamie Van Doren to play the role of Jerri Jordan. She's been promised it. She's screwed half of Hollywood, the slut. But I'm told you could fix it with a phone call." Then she started. She got a mouth like the fires of hell. She stopped and looked up at me. I'm nearly passing out and she said, "Can you help me, Mr Aspanu?"

'I said, "Call me Hector, my little Madonna, and don't worry, I fucking fix it, I swear to God." Then she smiled and said, "Well, I guess I better fix this, hey, Hector?" then she go to work. Never in all my life I ever had anything like it. She was the Devil's daughter. After she finished I made the phone call in front of her. They tell me Mamie Van Doren got the role. I tell them if Jayne Mansfield don't get the role I put the hit on the producer, director and Mamie Van fucking Doren as well, and also I invest money in da movie. Not 15 minutes later I get return call. Guess what? Miss Mansfield got the role, easy as that.

'After that I take Miss Mansfield to lunch. Jack White's Club, New York City. That night I fly her to Hollywood. We go dinner, dancing first, La Rue's Restaurant, Hollywood, then dancing Beverly Wilshire Hotel, then big room upstairs. She do the striptease dance for me and sit on my face. In the morning she go but she give me phone number. I give her mine in Sicily and contact number in New York. We kiss goodbye then I walk her downstairs and right in front of fucking hotel Mamie Van Doren get out of car screaming "You

fucking slut" and attack Miss Mansfield. Ha ha. Jayne big girl.
Pennsylvania farm girl, strong as the fucking ox. She punch
Mamie Van Doren out with two hits and leave her on the
fucking sidewalk. Then she kiss me goodbye and hop in taxi.

'We remain good friends right up to the day she died. Best
sex I ever had. I help her get lot of movies.

'I get her in Italian movies, all the fucking Hercules movies,
about four or five. This time she suck me twice as hard
because she want me to help her new boyfriend, whatever,
Micky Hargitay. Shit, in 1958 she even invite me to her
fucking wedding in Palos Verde, California, but I couldn't go.
She called me Poppa Aspanu or Uncle Hector or sometimes
Padrino. She tell me her father's name was Herbert and I
remind her of him, because he would give her anything, too.
The last movie I got her in was *Las Vegas Hillbillies* in 1966.
She was on her own and doing OK by then.'

Tommy Greco interrupted. 'She had her head cut off in a
car accident in California with Micky Hargitay, didn't she?'

Don Hector laughed. 'Everyone think this, even I make
joke about it. But, no, she died in car crash one night, 29 June
1967, on a road outside New Orleans. Micky Hargitay not
even in the car. Sam Brody driving. He died too and, no, she
never lost her head, only her blonde wig. She no stupid
bimbo, ya know,' said Don Hector. 'She went to University of
Texas and UCLA. She very smart, tough lady. She know who
to be friends with.'

Tommy Greco interrupted again. 'You ever met Marilyn
Monroe?'

'Yeah,' said the Don, 'but I never fuck her. She had the pox. Every gangster and big deal movie boss and politician in America fuck Monroe, all catch the pox. Fuckin' Kennedy give her the pox. She passed it on, but not to me. Out of 'em all, Jayne was the best but Monroe have more friends and do more favours, and had too much shit on too many people. She knew too much so a lot of people helped her, but then she had to go. She started saying get me this movie or I tell this to FBI, get me that movie or I tell this to Senate Committee. She started to become a fucking problem.'

Joey wanted to ask about the photos but bit his tongue.

Tommy Greco was fascinated. 'Kennedy, you ever meet Kennedy?' asked Tommy.

'Yeah,' said the Don. 'I know his poppa, old Joe. Old Joe use to do the business with Capone, that's how John F Kennedy got to meet Sam Giancana and I met his cocaine-snorting dragon of a wife as well.'

Tommy Greco nearly jumped out of his chair. 'What Jacqueline Kennedy? Jackie O? You met her? Jesus, she was beautiful.'

The old Don spat. 'Crazy-eyed, coke-snorting fucking mental case. Mansfield was close up beautiful, Kennedy was a coke addict, Monroe had the pox and a morphine habit, and Mamie Van Doren was a fucking big mouth and a drunk and a fucking lesbian. She do it with Monroe, Joe DiMaggio tell me.'

'What was Frank Sinatra like?' asked one of the boys.

'Ha ha,' laughed the Don, 'the Irish Sicilian. He was about

142

as Sicilian as that suit you're wearing, and correct me if I'm wrong but that was made in Milano by that Portofino faggot Frenchman.'

'Padrino,' said Joey, 'you said once Jayne Mansfield broke your heart. What happened?'

The old Don went quiet, then swallowed another glass of grappa. 'She divorced Hargitay in 1964 and I asked her to be my wife. She say no. She say I love you, Padrino, but no. I say why not and she was a bit drunk and say to me because she can't marry a man who looks like fucking Bela Lugosi.'

'Who was he?' asked Tommy.

'He was the guy who play the fucking vampire in the silent horror movies,' said the Don.

Joey was remembering the old photos and was dying to ask the fatal Kennedy question. But the Don looked at his watch and said, 'Come on, Joey, we go to Catania, we have long drive.'

After every man kissed him goodbye, Don Hector got in the car and said, 'Let's go, Joey.' As Joey drove away Don Hector said, 'That Tommy, he not a bad boy but we gonna have to bury him with Pietro. A pity really. By the way, young Joey, you got rid of all the photos, didn't you?'

'Yes, Padrino,' said Joey.

'Good boy,' said the Don.

But for some reason Joey felt the old man's eyes cutting into the back of his head and he felt a bit car sick.

Joey remembered the old Sicilian saying, 'Tell the hangman the truth and save the lies for the priest.'

He didn't feel too well at all.

Don Hector spoke to all gathered at La Casa Lupara Bianca, the house of the white shotgun. He spoke for a long time about the life and death of the great Sicilian bandit Salvatore Juiliano. He was working up to something.

Meanwhile, Luigi Monza sat outside with the other bodyguards. Today was the day Monza was to enter the clan Aspanu and become a full *Uomini Respattati*, or member of the clan. A Greek had been kidnapped from a ship in Palermo for no reason other than they needed someone to kill for the ceremony and the seaman had offended the sister of a fishmarket worker who was a member of the Lady of Sorrow's clan, an arm of the Aspanu clan that gave food and cash to the poor. The mafia's version of the Red Cross.

After the Don's ranting, rambling speech about the life of Salvatore Juiliano and the death and revenge of the traitors who betrayed him had finished, the facts of which had been altered slightly with each passing year, Monza was brought into the house by Di Tommaso and the Benozzo brothers.

The Greek seaman was brought in through another door, his hands tied behind his back. He didn't look happy.

'Men of the clan Aspanu, before you is Luigi Monza. He wishes to join our ranks, he has been told what must be done and what must be said, so now we wait.'

Don Hector nodded to Joey and he gave Monza a knife. Monza approached the terrified Greek and cut his throat from ear to ear. The body fell, then Monza bent down and pushed both his hands into the wound and covered his hands in the hot blood, then approached Don Hector and knelt before him and held out his blood-covered hands. The old Don took Monza's hands in his own and Monza spoke a solemn oath in Italian.

Don Hector helped Monza to his feet and then said to the men gathered the words one member uses when introducing a second member to a third member: '*La stessa cosa*', meaning 'a friend of ours'.

All the men gathered yelled, 'Bravo,' and took turns in shaking the blood-soaked hands of the new *Uomini Respattati*, and kissed him on both cheeks.

'This is the way it is done,' said Don Hector. 'This is the only way.'

CHAPTER 9

THE SLEEPING DOG

On the long flight home from Rome, Joey considered the myth and legend of Salvatore Juiliano. A man who from 1943 to 1950 had become a legend in Sicily. The legend varied, depending on what part of Sicily the stories were told. They couldn't even agree on his grave site. Tourists from all over the world brought flowers to the supposed tomb of the great Sicilian bandit legend, yet the real grave was at Montelepre. A man with two graves and even two names: Salvatore Giuliano or Salvatore Juiliano. The mainland Italian press called him Giuliano; the peasants called him Juiliano.

He was the Robin Hood of Sicily, but was he a hero or a murdering bandit? A man killed by the mafia, but whose padrino was a mafia godfather. The legend was a myth, a lie and a contradiction – but, as they say in Sicily, today's lie will become tomorrow's truth. The peasants couldn't read or write, but they believed the English legend of Robin Hood, and that Juiliano was the same. Juiliano had been a young, handsome murderer who created his own myth. He could read and write when others couldn't, and in the land of the blind the one-eyed man is king.

Then came Hector Aspanu, a man whose dark past went back before the war. It seems he too created his own myth from the blood of a thousand Sicilian lies. Who did order the death of Juiliano? Old Don Aspanu, Hector's mafia boss father, did he order Juiliano's death? And then in the name of honour and Sicilian revenge raise up against his own father and family?

Joey smiled and thought to himself it was a very evil and treacherous thing to think of his uncle but it was probably the perfect truth. In Sicily the smile of a friend conceals the eyes of an enemy and the Sicilian mafia had always been very good at killing their own friends and relatives and not so good at killing their enemies.

Joey laughed about the Sicilian legends. It was the same with the mafia. The Onorata Societa, La Cosa Nostra. Its whole fortune was based on Turkish morphine turned into heroin in Sicilian laboratories and sold worldwide to men, women and children condemned by the drug to horrific despair. And the men who pocket the money call themselves the men of honour, men of respect. It was all just a lie. The only truth is that the man holding the gun tells the man with no gun what is a lie and what is the truth. A child screaming for a hit of heroin knows only the truth of relief the needle can bring and will blindly agree with anything.

All these thoughts ran through Joey's head as the big jet droned homewards. It was all just a chess game of lies and blood. The only truth in it was to believe nothing when you fight on the side of the devil. Your greatest defence was to tell the world that God is with you. No war can ever be won or even entered into without two lies for every bullet. This was Joey's world and understanding it gave him comfort. His life depended on that understanding.

Meanwhile, back in Sicily, a group of Yank mafiosi were sitting in a cafe on the waterfront in the seaside village of Castellammare del Golfo. Present were Tommy Greco, Tony Rolli, Dominic Scarvaci, Ciccio Folizzi, Filippo Provenzano, Nick Morelli, Fannita Palazzolo and Guido Petrosino.

'Jesus,' said Tommy to Tony Rolli, 'one minute the old vampire kisses me and gives me his blessing, the next minute I get a call from New York to tell me I stay as I am and Rocco fucking Rolli, your cocksucker uncle, gets the nod. What the hell has he ever done?'

'He's killed a lot of people,' grunted Tony in his best hard-man style. Now that his uncle had been given the nod from Don Hector, Tony didn't feel the need to be so polite to Tommy fucking Greco.

'Yeah, but I've made the family more fucking money,' screamed Tommy.

As this childish show of sour grapes was going on inside the café, a 1959 Chrysler Royal pulled up outside. Luigi Monza,

Franco Di Tommaso and the Benozzo brothers got out of the car all carrying sawn-off shotguns. Each also had a loaded .45 automatic handgun in his belt. Benny had a second thought, put his Lupara back in the car and opened the boot and pulled out an old wartime German machine gun and checked it. Then Benny thought again, put the MP40 back in the boot and pulled out a fully automatic AR15 machine gun with a 30-round clip.

'Make up ya fucking mind, for Christ's sake,' snapped his brother Bobby.

Benny smiled. 'I'm OK now.'

As the four walked towards the café, Franco asked Luigi, 'Did Don Hector say just Tommy Greco, or everyone?'

'I forget,' said Luigi.

'Better be on the safe side,' said Franco.

'Yeah,' Luigi said agreeably. 'All of them, then.' He was never one for arguments over little things like wasting ammunition.

Melbourne, 1997. Joey Gravano, Tina Torre and a giant Lithuanian psychopath, Viko Radavic, sat quietly in the lounge bar of the Bagdad Hotel in Johnston Street, Abbotsford.

'I don't like your choice of pubs,' said Joey to Tina.

'But Cassie said to meet her here,' replied Tina.

Joey thought of Cassandra Connor, the cat in the birdcage girl, and the Collingwood crew's odd relationship with the Albanians. That's why he'd brought the big Lithuanian with him as a bodyguard.

'Did ya hear about the little dwarf who was standing in front of this pub last week?' said Joey.

Tina detected a joke and said, 'No. Go on, tell me.'

'Well,' said Joey, 'he was standing in front of the pub singing "21 today, 21 today" and a really big bloke walked by him and heard him singing and said to the little fella, "Shut up, you little turd, or I'll give you fucking 21, ya little prick." So the dwarf pulled out a tomahawk and smashed the big bloke across the left kneecap and the big fella fell to the sidewalk and the dwarf brained him with the tomahawk, dragged the dead body up the laneway behind the pub, put the tomahawk back under his coat and started singing "22 today, 22 today". Ha ha.'

Tina laughed, but big Viko Radavic was horrified.

'Jesus, I hope he isn't outside when we leave. Didn't anyone call the police?'

Joey and Tina looked at Viko and Tina said, poker-faced, 'No, Viko, I think he sings in front of a pub in Richmond now.'

'Thank God for that,' said Viko. 'I don't want trouble with any mad axe-carrying dwarf.'

Both Joey and Tina looked at each other. Viko was hired for size and physical violence, not for his sophisticated sense of humour. He was in no danger of being in the heavy-thinking brigade of the Melbourne criminal world.

As Viko sat quietly, no doubt pondering the thought of some insane dwarf axe murderer who sang in front of pubs, Tina started talking to Joey about movies.

A Johnny Cash song was playing behind the jump. It was 'Ghost Riders in the Sky'.

'Anyway,' said Tina, a little annoyed, 'are you listening?'

'Yeah,' said Joey, 'I'm listening.'

Tina continued her movie-trivia monologue when Viko interrupted again, raising his glass of vodka. '*Ish fay carter*,' said the big Lithuanian. Or something that sounded like it, anyway.

Joey raised his glass of whisky and said, '*La bar danna.*'

So, with all correct Lithuanian drinking formalities out of the way, Tina continued. She was a little frustrated.

'If it wasn't for George Raft, no one would ever have heard of Humphrey fucking Bogart,' she said, and away she went.

Joey couldn't care less about the movies, but Tina had a very interesting tactical and strategic point that he agreed with.

Just then, the big Lithuanian started laughing like a drain. 'Ha, ha, ha, ha,' Viko guffawed. 'That was joke! Ha ha ha.'

'What?' asked Tina icily, looking as if she'd like to hit him with a tomahawk. 'Humphrey Bogart or Montgomery Clift?'

'No,' said Viko, 'fucking dwarf with axe.'

Both Joey and Tina smiled and nodded patiently while the big Lithuanian sat laughing to himself and repeating, '21 today, 21 today. Ha ha. I like that. Ha ha.'

Then Viko beamed a large smile. 'My birthday yesterday.'

'Oh,' said Tina. 'Happy birthday, Viko.'

'Yes,' continued Viko, 'my wife give me root and pair of shoes.'

Joey and Tina were a bit comically shocked at this remark.

'That was nice of her,' said Tina, trying not to laugh.

'No, not really,' said Viko, 'they both too big!' He laughed, then said delightedly, 'I make joke too, ha ha.'

Joey and Tina laughed with him.

'Very good, Viko, very good,' said Tina.

Meanwhile, Joey made a mental note not to bring Viko drinking with him again. Paid insane killers should not be encouraged to accompany their betters on social outings.

As all this was going on, a 1950 Plymouth coupe pulled up outside the pub with Mark Dardo at the wheel, and Niko Ceka beside him holding the late Fracoz Lepetikha's Israeli-made .50-calibre automatic handgun.

'Micky Kelly said leave the Sicilian alive. Don't ask me why. Just pop the Lithuanian. He was the one who got Fracoz.'

Niko got out of the car and walked towards the pub door. Inside, Joey was telling another joke. And the music behind the bar changed from Johnny Cash to the magic sound of Dick Dale, king of the surf guitar.

'Oh, a bit of the old *Pulp Fiction* music. I like that movie,' Viko said, interrupting Joey's joke.

'Yes, yes, yes,' said Joey impatiently. 'We've all seen it. Do ya want to hear this fuckin' joke or what?'

'Yes,' said Tina.

Viko went silent. He half-realised he was doing the wrong thing. Joey continued, 'There was this Irish guy who appeared in court recently and got 12 months' jail for fucking a goat.'

'And,' interrupted Viko delightedly, 'his little brother get 18 months' jail for acting the goat. Ha ha. Everyone know this joke.'

'That's it,' said Joey, really annoyed. 'This is the last time we bring this retard out drinking with us, Tina. Bodyguard or no bodyguard.'

'Who you call retard, you little dago pipsqueak?' said Viko.

'You, ya big drongo,' said Joey.

'If your wife not here, I snap your neck, fucking Sicilian shitkicker,' said Viko.

'Don't push it too far,' said Joey, reaching for his gun.

'Ha ha ha,' laughed Viko. 'Mafia couldn't win war with girls' school volleyball team.'

'That's it!' yelled Joey, going for his gun just as Niko Ceka opened the door of the lounge and aimed the barrel of the big automatic at the big Lithuanian's head.

Tina screamed, '*Ruberia*, Joey! *Ruberia!*'

She thought the hotel was being robbed, and was screaming 'Robbery!' in Italian. Joey pulled out his .38 police special revolver and aimed at the door and fired almost at the same time as the Albanian squeezed the trigger on the big automatic, letting off three massive blasts. Two of which missed, but the third hit Viko Radavic full in the face. A hole the size of a fingertip appeared in his left cheekbone and a hole the size of a golfball blew out the back of his head. The giant staggered up, screaming and charging at the door before he dropped.

Joey pulled the trigger of his .38 twice as he grabbed Tina and threw her to the floor. One slug smashed into Niko Ceka's chest, but the giant Lithuanian got in Joey's line of fire as he charged his attacker. The Albanian backed away, wounded, and let three more rounds go full into the massive chest of Viko Radavic.

The Lithuanian fell forward and brought the Albanian down with him. Joey grabbed Tina and they ran out the back door. Mark Dardo jumped out of the old Plymouth coupe, dragged the Lithuanian off the screaming Niko and helped him to his feet. Niko Ceka said, 'Give me your gun,' and Mark handed over his .45 automatic and Niko emptied the clip of seven rounds into the giant's body.

'You're hit,' said Mark.

'Yeah,' said Niko, 'fucking dago dog shot me, Draco.'

'Come on,' said Mark Dardo, 'we get you to the doctor. I know one in Footscray.'

As the Albanians drove away, Viko Radavic opened his eyes and laughed weakly, the death rattle in his throat. 'Ha, ha, ha, 21 today.' Some sense of humour.

CHAPTER 11

THE WINK

I've got lawyers, guns and money. I'll live forever. Ha ha
CHRISTOPHER DALE FLANNERY

It was 1997 and Joey's second trip to America in the same year. Uncle Hector had a bee in his bonnet again. It was not Joey's idea of a good time. Nor his bride's, come to that. Although Tina never mentioned the word 'mafia', she did ask, 'Was Viko Radavic in the bricklaying business as well, Joey?'

It was a fair question. Poor Tina had witnessed three serious acts of violence since knowing Joey and these flights overseas, on which she wasn't invited, placed a strain on a marriage that Joey held dear.

Tina had other disappointments. She had to admit, for instance, that possibly Cassie Connor may no longer be the dear friend she thought she once was. Cassie had said she was ringing from a mobile phone in Footscray, but she had in fact made the date to meet at the Bagdad Hotel in Abbotsford from the Men's Gallery Club in Hobart. The whole thing was a Micky Kelly set-up with the Albanians to get poor Viko as a payback for Fracoz. The last time Joey had been to New York, it was as a personal favour for Peppie Pisciotta, Gotti's underboss. Pisciotta was a member of the Aspanu clan, even though he was a made guy in Gotti's family, the old Gambino family. Joey was to be met at Kennedy Airport by his dickhead cousin Fat Sally Gigante. Joey was all airported out, as he seemed to spend half his life in them, and they all started seeming the same …

The guy in the seat in front of him was trying to run his hand up the legs of a fantastic-looking red-haired hostess, and she was trying to be polite. Joey, being the right-thinking married man he now was, got out of his seat and reached around and gave the yuppie with the wandering hands a sharp backhander. 'Behave yourself, ya bum.'

The posh passenger altered his Mardi Gras attitude and got solemn, sorry and serious in a second flat. Joey got back in his seat. The smile of gratitude the hostess beamed at Joey was pure champagne, but Joey only wanted to have a nap, not a chat. He put on his headphones, flicked the little switch to country music and went to sleep. He reminded himself Uncle Hector would ring him in that restaurant in Times Square. What was it called? He had to kill someone. Uncle Hector would tell him who.

New York was a toilet bowl as far as Joey was concerned. He was collected at the airport by some mob guy named Charlie Fontana, who couldn't speak a word of understandable Italian, nor English for that matter. He was a comic-book gangster clown, wearing dark glasses and a fucking tuxedo and, believe it or not, a Fedora hat. Joey felt quite embarrassed to even be seen walking with him.

Fontana took Joey to a 1984 black Cadillac Deville. Joey had a reservation at the Waldorf Astoria, but his dickhead cousin had cancelled it and booked Joey a room in some shithole motel in the Bronx.

'Well, you can bash that up ya bum for a start,' said Joey. 'Take me to the Waldorf.'

'But Sally said he...' Fontana protested before Joey backhanded him across the mouth. Jetlag had not improved his mood.

'Take me to the fucking Waldorf and tell that son of a bitch I'll meet him in Times Square. Get him to ring me at the Waldorf. No one stays at the Bronx. You bury dead dogs in the Bronx – you don't stay overnight there. This is a fucking insult and you can tell Sally I said so. OK, shithead?'

'Yes, Mr Gravano,' said Charlie.

'And take that stupid fucking hat off, you imbecile. You look like Al Capone's brother-in-law. Jesus Christ, no wonder the Colombians fucked you all up the arse. You're all too busy doing Humphrey Bogart impersonations.'

Joey liked to stay at the Waldorf. It had history. The Gallo brothers shot Albert Anastasia in the barber shop of the

Waldorf. His uncle Hector used to get Jayne Mansfield to kiss the rabbit at the Waldorf. They made a good salad too. All the old mob guys stayed at the Waldorf. The place was a monument to mob history. And the Bronx sucked.

His cousin was a fucking idiot and, as for stupid Charlie with the funny hat, the fool had spent the drive from the airport to the hotel telling Joey about some insane hijacking of a truckload of fucking Calvin Klein underwear from the airport, and the truckload of underwear got hijacked off them by Johnny Spatolla and his crew and got sold to the Hudson county crew in New Jersey. There was gonna be a sit-down over this, as Johnny Spatolla and his crew had fucked up ... and, by the way, did Joey want a girl?

Charlie had the number of a mob-run escort service that hired off-duty international air hostesses only, real top shelf. Joey took the number and promised to tell the lady on the phone he was a friend of Charlie Batts. Evidently the idiot driver was also a part-time pimp.

New York, thought Joey, as he checked in to the Waldorf and went up to his room. They all watch too much television. The whole town was a Disneyland for wannabe gangsters. He expected Quentin Tarantino to jump out at any moment and yell, 'Cut! Can we try that again, but this time with feeling?' New York was a city where life desperately imitated art, and the art wasn't much in the first place. There was something surreal about the place.

Joey looked at the name and phone number Charlie the driver had given him. Decided to shower and sleep first, then ring it. His fool of a cousin could wait. This is the fucking twilight zone, he thought. This is Gotham City. He headed for the bathroom with the Waldorf's complimentary bottle of Suntory Whisky. He'd flown all the way to America to get a free bottle of Japanese whisky, he thought to himself.

Joey showered and with the help of his complimentary bottle of Suntory he slept solidly and awoke at approximately nine o'clock that night. He decided to ring his uncle in Palermo to find out what he was meant to be doing in New York, and who to. For a highly organised criminal network, things could be quite disorganised at times. After being told off by his uncle, and shocked at the coded instructions given, he received a phone call from Fat Sally and arranged to meet him at the Gotham Health Club, New Jersey.

He hung up only to be rung back by Fat Sally to say that he had to attend some family trouble in Monro Street, Hoboken, and later a sit-down at the Park Avenue Athletic Club, again in New Jersey. But he would be at the Little Sicily Club in Knickerbocker Avenue in Brooklyn by 1pm, and would Joey like to meet him there? Joey smelled a rat and, considering Uncle Hector's phone call, said no. Sally then said he had other stop-offs where he could meet Joey. Jackson Street, Hoboken? The Crystal Ballroom, Hoboken? Joey didn't like all these come over to Jersey hints. Not at all.

'Look,' said Joey, 'I thought we was gonna meet in Times Square at the Times Square Brewery Restaurant. What's with all this come to Jersey, the Bronx and Brooklyn bullshit?'

Then Sally broke down. 'What's going on, Joey?' he whimpered. 'What have I done to upset Don Hector? Please, Joey.'

Joey knew Sally was a little bit paranoid. 'Look, Sal,' said Joey, 'in this world there are two kinds of ants – soldier ants and piss ants – and you're a fucking piss ant. In other words, don't get paranoid, because, in the end, Sal, ya just not that fucking important. OK, cousin?'

Sally was offended but, strangely enough, the insult put him at ease.

'Relaxio,' said Joey. 'Ya got nothing to worry about.'

'OK,' said Sally. 'Thanks, Joey.'

'Times Square tomorrow. OK, buddy?' said Joey.

'OK,' said Sally. 'See ya.'

Joey hung up. Poor Sally, he thought. I'm no fucking rocket scientist but, compared to Sally, I'm a fucking genius. He made two more phone calls, one to a gunsmith named Bruno Brunelleschi, who ran a Mexican restaurant on Eighth Avenue, not all that far from Madison Square Garden. He would deliver the correct firearm, a nice clean throwaway.

The second call was to the number Charlie had given him. After explaining that he was a friend of Charlie Batts he was shocked when the woman on the other end of the phone cooed, 'Oh, certainly, Mr Gravano. We have been expecting your call. We have a lovely lady, an English girl named Donna. She will be in a cab and at the Waldorf in 15 minutes. Oh, and by the way, Mr Gravano, there will be no charge. Donna is available for however long you like. Mr Batts will take care of the expense. I do hope you enjoy your stay in New York.'

Well, thought Joey, the funny-hat gangster did something right. Joey then ordered up a little room service.

'Hello, do you have any non-Japanese whisky available? Yeah, good. Well, send up a bottle of French champagne and Irish whiskey – that's one of each,' said Joey. You had to explain things slowly to Americans in case they sent up a bottle of champagne and whiskey mixed together in the same bottle. Five minutes later room service arrived with a magnum bottle of 'French' champagne, but a quick glance at the fine print revealed it a product of Israel. The large bottle of Irish whiskey was a product of Mexico.

Fifteen minutes after the booze was delivered, there was a knock on the door. He opened it to find a strangely familiar face belonging to a raunchy-looking redhead with a sparkling smile and green eyes. The same redhead hostie he had helped on the flight over.

'Well, well, well,' she purred in a posh English accent, 'I was hoping I might catch you on the flight back. I checked and found out you'd booked a return ticket. My name is Donna Allen, Mr Gravano,' she said, holding out her hand. Joey shook it.

'Please come in,' said Joey. The gorgeous woman walked in and Joey shut the door and locked it.

'I'm told, Mr Gravano, that I'm to treat you as a VIP, and that the cost will be taken care of by others. So, in other words, I'm all yours for as long as you like. I'm in New York on a four-day layover, then it's back to London.'

Joey didn't know what to say. He asked her if she wanted a drink.

'Champagne,' said Donna.

She was wearing a very expensive, well-cut black suit with skirt, stockings and high heels. She looked bloody fantastic. As she polished off one glass of champagne Joey poured her another and she skolled that back. Then held her glass out for another refill.

'Mr Gravano, I'm afraid…'

'Please call me Joey,' he interrupted.

'Well, Joey, I must warn you that, after three to four glasses of champagne, I just have to get out of my things. You don't mind, do you?'

'No,' said Joey, 'certainly not.'

The third glass was polished off and refilled and the redhead removed her suit jacket to reveal a substantial set of tits held up in a black lace bra. She polished off her fourth glass and was promptly poured a fifth. She then reached around with her left hand while holding her full champagne glass in her right and undid a button and a zip. Her skirt fell to the floor and she stepped out of it. She was wearing high-cut black lace knickers and black stockings and black stiletto high heels. She downed her fifth glass, gave a little burp, giggled and said, 'Pardon me. Well, Mr Gravano, I mean Joey, I'm afraid after five glasses of champagne I tend to misbehave myself terribly.'

She then reached her hands around behind her back and undid her bra and let loose her spectacular tits. They weren't watermelons, but a big improvement on grapefruit. She then took off her knickers.

'Would you like me to leave my stockings and high heels on?' she asked.

Joey nodded. He felt calmer than this before he shot somebody.

'Well, Joey, I think it's high time I met your one-eyed friend. Would you like to make the introductions?'

She seemed impressed. 'Oh, my goodness,' she exclaimed, dropping to her knees. 'I'm afraid you'll think me a shocking slut, Mr Gravano, I mean Joey, but I'm sure I can rely on your discretion. Would you mind terribly if I…'

Joey knew what she meant. 'No,' said Joey. 'Not at all.'

'Oh, and by the way,' said Donna, 'I'm a good girl, but, if you wish to mistreat me if I do anything to displease you, then I fully expect verbal abuse and a little physical chastisement.'

Joey had met this kind of masochistic whore before, and he went along with it. He gave her a slap across the face with his open right hand and grunted, 'You talk too much, slut.'

Her eyes went wild. Joey took off his belt. If this is the way she wanted it, that's the way she'd get it. He was an obliging chap, at heart. He knew the script she was working to.

'Come on, whore, do it, do it!'

The woman was moaning with lust, then Joey snarled, 'Stop it. Get up and bend over the bed. You're a filthy slut, a nice English girl like you whoring her arse like some crack addict slag. You should be ashamed of yourself. Bend over.'

She bent over. 'Yes, I know I'm a filthy whore,' she

whispered. 'I can't help it. I feel so ashamed, my parents didn't raise me for this.'

Joey let go with a welt across her bare buttocks that made her squeal. 'You're one sick bitch, Donna,' snarled Joey.

She threw herself back on the bed and spread her legs wide open and her hips raised up. 'Come on, Joey, make me scream some more. Come on, baby.'

Joey mounted and humped her like a mad bull while she sank her teeth deep into his shoulder. 'You're one sick puppy, Donna,' he said.

The woman laughed. 'You love it, Joey. I saw the look in your eyes. You liked hitting me. Go on, admit it,' said Donna. 'It turned you on, didn't it?'

It was true, but Joey couldn't bring himself to admit it.

'Go on, you wimp dago – do it properly,' she spat. 'I'm terribly disappointed, Joey, I thought you Italians knew how to handle a woman.'

'Shut up, you sick whore,' he snapped. He was no longer in the mood for this masochistic bullshit. 'Get out, ya fucking psycho,' he snarled.

But she just stood there, smiling at him.

'Joey, you're nothing but a wimp faggot and no wonder you have to pay for it, you pickle-headed ponce.'

The punch caught her on the point of the jaw, and she folded up like a deck of cards. He rang the escort agency and told them to come and get her before he threw her out the window.

When Charlie Fontana the comic-book gangster turned up next morning, he was dressed in a more normal way – grey double-breasted suit with a white shirt, open-neck collar and Italian slip-on shoes. He looked like an off-duty nightclub tout instead of a complete joke.

Joey was carrying a small .22-calibre magnum revolver with a threaded barrel and silencer. He had the revolver in his right coat pocket and the silencer in his left. When they got to the restaurant he could tell that both Sally and Charlie were armed up. It's hard to conceal shoulder holsters, even under a well-cut suit jacket. The restaurant was crowded.

'Jesus, Joey,' said Charlie, 'that English girl Donna is a case. She wants your phone number.'

'You're kidding,' grunted Joey.

'No. For real, Joey. She's in love. Reckons you gave her the best time she's ever had.'

Joey couldn't believe this. 'That sheila's a fucking mental case,' he said dismissively, then turned his attention to Sally. 'Now,' he said, 'what's all this paranoid shit from you? Who said Uncle Hector was upset with you? You wanna keep ya fucking nose out of the cocaine, Sal, it's rattling ya fucking brain.'

For some reason Joey's pissed-off attitude put Sally at his ease.

'Yeah, I'm sorry, Joey. I should have known better. I was just freaking out over bullshit.'

'Damn right,' said Joey, 'if the Don wanted you whacked he'd just ring ya and tell ya to shoot yourself, ya stupid prick.'

All three men laughed, then Joey decided to lighten up on poor Charlie. 'Where did ya get that crazy redhead nympho, Charlie?

Charlie talked fast while the going was good. 'She has the same arrangement with an escort service in London, Sydney and, I think, Rome or Tokyo, and I heard she's done work in the Netherlands. She's the sickest pain freak we have ever had on the books. And holy shit, Mr Gravano, she fell in love with you. When we got her back to the agency, she was in love.'

'Who's this?' interrupted Sally.

'Some posh la-di-dah whore, English air hostess Charlie fixed me up with,' replied Joey.

'Sucked more dummies than a millionaire's baby and a dead-set, crazy pain freak. She likes it hard, fast and very, very rough. Any rougher and you'd have to kick her to death.'

'Jesus, Charlie,' said Sally, 'introduce me.'

'I will,' said Charlie, 'but she's on the plane tonight, won't be back for six weeks, I think it's Sydney next, then back home to London, then she returns to New York.'

'Well, fucking ring me when she gets in next,' said Sally.

'There's a place near here,' said Charlie, 'a girlie bar that puts on a good show.'

Sally smiled at Charlie. 'Ya mean Mad Dog's?'

'Yeah,' said Charlie. 'You remember the porno queen Vanessa Del Rio? Well, she puts on a strip at Mad Dog's every afternoon. Ya gotta see this to believe it.'

'Well,' said Joey, 'What are we waiting for?'

'By the way,' asked Sally, 'what did Don Hector want, Joey?'

'It can wait,' said Joey. 'You know the Don, a lot of fuss over very little.'

'Yeah,' replied Sally with a giggle, 'that's Uncle Hector all over. Hurry up and wait.'

'Yeah,' said Joey. 'He's an old man so I humour him.'

Sally nodded. He was at his ease now.

'Hey, Fontana,' said Joey.

'Yes, Mr Gravano.'

'Call me Joey, OK, Charlie?'

Charlie beamed a big smile. 'OK, Joey.'

'Yeah, don't mind me. I got a senile uncle, jet lag and a stomach ulcer,' said Joey. 'So let's see this striptease porno queen.'

The three men got up and walked out.

Mad Dog's strip joint was in Times Square and the star attraction was Vanessa Del Rio, one of the most awesome, outrageous and spectacular bosomed and buttocked, trouser-swelling nymphos ever to come out of Puerto Rico. She was a dark-skinned, exotic smorgasbord of witchcraft. She'd retired from films, but was still earning big money for a striptease performance only she could put on.

As the three men entered the dark club the loud throb of strip music hit them. The room was filled with men and the smell of stale tobacco smoke, stale booze, vomit, piss and perfume. The stage was set about two feet off the floor and customers could reach out and stuff money into the garters Vanessa Del Rio wore high on both legs. She was naked except for stiletto heels, and her body glistened in a mixture of sweat and baby oil. Her garters were stuffed with tens, twenties and some 100-dollar bills.

Vanessa balanced on her arse with her legs spread, lifted her hips off the stage, spread her legs wider than the Grand Canyon and did her trick with a vibrator that would scare a water buffalo. Joey had shot men with sawn-off shotguns that were smaller. It was more a freak show than a sex show.

It was not what turned Joey on, but it had its good points, professionally speaking. In the darkness Fat Sally and Charlie stood in front of Joey like Beavis and Butthead, totally transfixed. Joey took the little handgun out of his right pocket and the silencer out of his left and threaded it on, then put the barrel to the back of Charlie's skull in the darkness and – pop. The music muffled the click of the hammer as it slammed down. Believe it or not Sally didn't even notice when Charlie fell to the floor. Then Joey tapped Sally on the shoulder. Sally turned, and in the darkness Joey winked at him.

'What's up, cousin?' asked Sally.

Joey winked again, then shot Sally in the guts.

As Sally gulped air and doubled over Joey put the barrel to his head and pulled the trigger twice more.

As Joey turned to walk out he noticed a crowd girl looking at him – a whore who worked the crowd. As Joey walked by the stunned girl, he said, 'Sorry, honey,' then shot her in the head. She wouldn't have made much of a witness, but in the sleazy, smoke-filled darkness she was the only one to notice and that made her, for better or worse, a witness. Which made her dead.

Outside, Joey walked down the street talking to himself. 'Yeah, well, Sally. Ya told me to give ya the wink first. Ya can't get much fairer than that. Sorry, cousin.'

CHAPTER 12

BRONCO BILLY

As Billy Joe fell to the floor, the crowd all gathered
around and wondered at his final words:
'Don't take your guns to town, son. Leave your guns at home;
Leave your guns at home, Bill. Don't take your guns to town.'
JOHNNY CASH

Tina Torre walked quietly along Peel Street, North Melbourne, after doing her early-morning shopping at the Queen Victoria Market. She was now married to a wealthy man and didn't have to shop for bargains at the market, but old habits die hard.

It was a cold, crisp morning and Tina was wearing a tracksuit and joggers as she lugged her bags and parcels to her Mercedes. She was planning to sell the Merc because Princess

Diana had died in one like it. Tina was very upset over the death of the Princess. It was strange, that. When all those poor people were murdered by that mentally retarded faggot in Tasmania the year before, Tina had been shocked, but not sad. But for some reason the death of the Princess really got to her. It was such a silly way to go, almost slapstick in its tragedy. An English princess, an Arab millionaire, a Welsh bodyguard and a French chauffeur filled with Scotch whisky, all in a German car. As Joey had said, the only thing that was missing was the Irish motor mechanic. And, if so, who was he working for: the IRA or MI6?

The world was starting to become a crazy place. Tina wanted Joey to stay home more. She didn't dare mention his business affairs, but she was no fool. As a Sicilian herself she recognised the formal Scarchi Sicilian manner in which Joey's uncle Hector was treated and greeted at the wedding.

Then there was the small matter of 60 men all carrying machine guns and shotguns in full view as the wedding procession left the church and headed through the streets of Palermo towards the Messina Club for the reception.

In fact, the wedding made *The Godfather* look like *The Sound of Music*. Tina's family couldn't help noticing it as well. The name Aspanu was almost as famous in Sicily as Juiliano himself.

Tina wanted to talk to Joey about a few things. First on the list was that she was pregnant and he didn't know yet. The doctor had confirmed it the day Princess Di was killed. Yes, Joey was to become a father and a family man himself, and

Tina's wish was that all this flying all over the world on the wishes and whims of the old vampire in Palermo would stop. But culture, tradition and habits die hard. She was a liberated woman, but she was foremost an Italian girl married to a very Italian man. She just couldn't say, 'Excuse me, my darling, I'm having a baby, so you will have to resign from the mafia?' It didn't work like that.

Tina got to her car, opened it, put away her parcels and got in. She was thinking about the baby. Surely it would slow Joey down, she thought contentedly.

That thought was the last thing that went through her mind, if you don't count the back window of the car. Because when she turned the key in the ignition every bit of Tina above her knees was blown to bits.

Benny Shapiro turned to Marven Mendelsohn as they stood in Victoria Street, North Melbourne, a hundred yards from the exploding Mercedes.

'Ya see,' said Benny seriously, 'that's what one landmine can do when it's rigged up correctly. I told ya the anti-tank gun would be sheer overkill.'

Marven nodded. 'But we use the anti-tank gun next time, hey?'

'Promise,' said Benny. 'The next time we use the anti-tank gun.'

'What sort of landmine was that?' asked Marven. 'M14 or M16?'

'No,' said Benny. 'Stock standard Israeli APM.'

'Hmmm,' mumbled Marven, 'do we have many of them?'

'I had three,' said Benny. 'Got two left now. But I do have a dozen boxes of mark 2 para flares right out of the Paynes Wessex factory, and a dozen Very pistols and a thousand flares.'

'A Very pistol?' said Marven.

'The old-style flare guns. They're hard to get, but they'd burn an elephant to death, them flares. Burn white hot under water.'

'Why do they call it a Very pistol?' asked Marven.

'Because it's very fucking painful,' laughed Benny.

Meanwhile, Simone Tao was getting off a plane at Tullamarine Airport, where her pal Joey was waiting for her. Simone had flown in from Hong Kong. It would be her last flight from her old home. She'd remained to wave goodbye to the British but, even though her new Chinese communist masters were all smiles, Simone felt a little ill at ease. Her links with the triads, not to mention various Italian and American crime families, had not gone totally unnoticed in certain circles. Always a forward planner, she had already sexually serviced one Chinese communist military commander and two high-ranking party members, not to mention a list of communist party financial and tax investigators. So there were lots of bonkers in Honkers, but she still wasn't sure all was well for her there. Something told her never to go back.

She was travelling to Melbourne on a return ticket, but she had no intention of returning.

She would leave behind half her wealth, but that still left her with almost two million dollars. One million invested in Australia with Joey in the heroin trade, and another million with the Don in the arms business. All the Aspanu money was safe in Swiss banks. Not to mention various other accounts all over the world.

Of course, in their lines of business, anything could go wrong at any time.

For instance, at that very moment, as Joey greeted her, he was unaware that his wife had been blown to pieces a few minutes earlier.

Now, Joey was one hard hombre, but had he known about Tina's bad luck with the bomb he may not have driven Simone straight to the Hilton Hotel, rushed her upstairs to a luxury apartment and got her clothes off for a bit of old times' sake. Simone was hardly through the door of the suite when Joey had his favourite weapon out and was ripping Simone's dress off. As Simone helped him into the master bedroom and fell back on the bed, wrapping her bare legs around him, she said, 'So, Joey. How's married life?'

The response to this made her give a little yelp.

Benny Shapiro was arguing with Marven Mendelsohn. 'Look, Micky said to leave the Sicilian alive. Anyway, they are on the bloody seventh floor. You can't hit the whole seventh floor with an anti-tank gun.'

'I can if you find out what fucking window to aim at,' grumbled Marven.

The two Jews were sitting in the street below the Hilton in Marven's 1954 Studebaker Landcruiser.

'Look,' said Benny, 'Micky wants us to kidnap the Chinese chick, OK? No one said nothing about hitting the fucking Hilton with a fucking anti-tank gun.'

'Well, this is giving me the shits!' yelled Marven. 'What's the use of having an anti-tank gun if we never get to use it.'

'Where's Pauline fucking Hanson when ya need some fish and chips?' replied Benny, laughing.

Marven stopped dead in his mental tracks.

'What the fuck has she got to do with the argument?' he asked.

'Well,' said Benny, 'there's more than one fish and chip shop in Australia and, believe me, Marven, you will get to use your bloody anti-tank gun soon enough.'

'You're a strange man, Benny,' replied Marven, which was pretty rich coming from him. 'Speaking of fish and chips, I'm hungry. Let's get something to eat, hey, Benny?'

'Yeah,' said Benny, 'we'll grab the gook tonight.'

As Marven drove away, Benny said, 'Did ya hear what old Pop Kelly said about Pauline Hanson?'

'Nah, what?' said Marven.

'Pop Kelly reckons he hopes the abos grab all the bloody land they can get their bloody hands on.'

'Fair dinkum,' replied Marven, puzzled.

'Yeah,' said Benny, 'because the more land the abos grab the less land there will be for the fucking Japanese, according to Pop.'

Benny roared laughing, but Marven looked quite serious. 'Ya know, Benny, silly as it sounds, old Pop's got a good point.' Mark Dardo and Niko Ceka sat quietly drinking in the Builders Arms Hotel in Fitzroy. Niko had been out of hospital only a few days and was still coughing up blood. He didn't look good. Shadows under his eyes, and as skinny as buggery. But he was cheerful, in spite of the fact the bullet Joey put into Niko's chest in the wild shoot 'em up at the Bagdad Hotel in Abbotsford had done more damage than was first thought.

The backyard doctor in Footscray had done the best he could. He removed the slug, then stuck an iron spike deep in the wound and rushed him to hospital, with a tall tale that Niko had been the victim of a totally unprovoked street attack.

The police were called, but Niko could not help them with the identification of his attackers except to say that they were Vietnamese. The funny thing was, Niko and his lawyers were going to lodge a crimes compensation application.

The doctors said the iron spike went in one side and out the other like a bullet, but they couldn't explain the internal damage. It was as if someone had been probing around inside the victim's chest with a pair of pliers. Very puzzling for the medical profession, it was.

Nevertheless, they concluded Niko appeared to be the innocent victim of a criminal attack and, as such, fully entitled to compo. One thing was for sure, he wasn't faking being crook.

'It will all turn out for the best,' Mark Dardo said to Niko, who was coughing up some more blood into a clean white tissue.

'Where's Micky Kelly? Why can't we kill that fucking Gravano?' said Niko.

'Ha ha,' laughed Mark. 'The Jews blew his wife up this morning, and I think they are on some mad mission either today or tonight.'

'Where's Micky?' said Niko.

'Calm down,' said Mark. 'He'll be here soon. Have another whisky, brother.'

As Niko polished off his fourth glass of whisky, Micky Kelly walked into the bar.

'How's it going, boys?' he said.

The Albanians greeted him with smiles all round and big hellos.

'Listen,' said Kelly, 'I've got Billy Jecka in the car outside. Do ya mind if I bring him in for a drink?'

'Bronco Billy,' said Mark Dardo.

Niko Ceka looked at his cousin Mark, and shrugged. 'Why not?' said Niko.

Mark looked at Micky.

'Oh, well, the more Albanians the better. Bronco hates Jews, so we best keep him clear of Benny and Marven.'

'Yeah,' said Micky, 'but he hates Germans worse. When Gravano hears about his wife he will attack. The fucking Calabrians won't back him against the Albanians, but he's been doing big business with the neo-Nazi crew from St Kilda.'

'Kaltenbrunner,' said Mark.

'Yeah,' replied Micky.

'Ernst fucking Kaltenbrunner,' said Niko, 'the fucking German gunsmith. He's almost as mad as Bronco Billy.'

'Yeah,' said Micky. 'So I thought we would get Billy in on it. I got Hacker Harris to ring Bronco.'

'Jesus,' said Mark Dardo. 'Hacker Harris. We are entering the land of the seriously insane now, aren't we?'

'Nah,' said Micky with a grin. 'Hacker is OK, and Bronco Billy and his team would go to the grave on Hacker's say-so. Believe me, when that fucking Sicilian finds out about his wife, it will be on.'

'He must know by now,' said Niko.

Micky Kelly smiled. 'Not according to the Jews. He's still in the Hilton with the Chinese moll. Benny and Marven will grab her tonight. Remove her, and the balance of their financial thinking will collapse. Joey's logic will shatter when he finds out about his wife. It will be total insanity by either tonight or tomorrow morning.'

'OK,' said Mark. 'Tell Bronco to come in. Let's work this out now.'

Micky smiled. 'I love this shit. I really love it.'

Ernst Kaltenbrunner was the grandson of a German war criminal, a former SS officer with the same name. The young Kaltenbrunner was a group leader of the Aryan Defence League and controlled a small army of approximately 200 neo-Nazi skinheads as well as operating as a backyard gunsmith and arms dealer. He'd heard and seen a lot of angry people, but nothing like Joey Gravano.

When Joey rang the Nazi at home in Horne Street, Elsternwick, he was nearly mad with grief and rage.

'I need your help, I'll pay anything,' he was sobbing. 'I fucking can't rely on my own people. None of 'em want a war with the Aussies and the fucking Albanians.'

Ernst had heard tell of the car bomb, and had been expecting Joey's call. '*Juden schwein*,' said Ernst, or something like that.

'What?' said Joey.

'Jewish pigs,' said Ernst. 'The *schwein* who did your wife, they were *Juden hunds*.'

'What?' said Joey.

'Jewish dogs,' replied Ernst.

'Speak English!' screamed Joey.

Then Ernst yelled down the phone in German something like: '*Ich werde den hund den kopf abschneiden*.'

'What?' cried Joey.

'I'll cut the dogs head off,' said Ernst.

'When?' yelled Joey.

'Tomorrow,' replied Ernst, 'but *geld zuerst*, Joey.'

'What?' said Joey, 'talk fucking English.'

'Money first,' replied the German. 'I'm not running a public fucking charity, OK?'

'OK,' said Joey grimly.

And that's how it began.

The following night at the Albanian Club in Yarraville, Bronco Billy Jecka and his team were drinking with Mark

Dardo, Niko Ceka and their crew. Micky Kelly was in attendance with his assorted gathering of Collingwood madmen. Kelly had also recruited the help of a Maltese crew, led by a mean-looking heavyweight kickboxer named Maltese Dave, who was there with his girlfriend, a stripper called Jasmyn.

'Ya won't believe this,' said Micky Kelly to Dardo, 'but Jasmyn here used to go out with bloody Gorgeous George Marcus. She knows 'em all. That's how Dave met her, on some weird plane trip to Italy. George had kidnapped her on some mad holiday to fucking Sicily and Big Dave took her off the plane in Rome. She knows 'em all. Gravano, Guglameno, Giordano, Capone, Monnella, the whole crew.'

Niko broke into the conversation. 'Do ya reckon Gravano will try hitting us tonight? I wish Benny and Marven was here.'

'No,' said Micky. 'They are with the Chinese slut. They've got her tucked up in some house in Avoca Street over in South Yarra.'

'What are they doing with her?' asked Mark.

'I think they are teaching her to speak Yiddish,' replied Micky, who fancied himself as a bit of a wit.

'If Joey or that fucking Nazi show tonight it's going to be one hell of a stink,' said Mark, 'especially when he thinks the Jews are here.'

'You want him to show?' asked Niko.

'Yeah,' said Micky, 'this is what it's all about, boys. Total rock and roll. Sneaking about, blowing the shit out of each other is OK, but in the end it comes down to this. High noon in front of the Red Dog saloon.'

Neither Niko nor Mark understood exactly what Micky meant by this crazy cowboy stuff. But they got his drift.

Outside the Albanian Club, Joey Gravano and a handful of brother Sicilians of the no-spika-da-English variety pulled up in a 1968 Chevy Impala. Behind them came the German, Ernst Kaltenbrunner, and three of his right-hand men in a 1966 Dodge Phoenix. Then came a 1970 Holden Monaro GTS, with five more neo-Nazis, and a 1967 Ford Fairmont with six men in it. A total of 20 men, all armed.

However, they had been misinformed a little about the reception committee in attendance. For instance, they were ignorant about a gang of 37 knife-carrying Maltese mental cases who happened to be in the club. Nor did they know that Micky Kelly and his crew and Bronco Billy and Mark Dardo's crews were inside. Joey was simply given to believe that Benny and Marven and a handful of Albanians were inside having a drink.

'Let's kill the *Juden schwein*,' said Ernst.

'For a start,' said Joey, 'when we walk in try to speak English for Christ's sake. I can't understand a word you're saying half the time.'

'OK,' said the blond psychopath, whose eyes were the palest, craziest Gestapo blue, like the Slyboy's.

'Yeah, well, *danke, mein herr*, as they say in the fucking German,' said Joey as he pulled out his .38-calibre police special.

His quiet Sicilian mates also produced handguns. Ernst produced a 9mm wartime Luger, but none of his men had guns – only iron bars and German army bayonets.

'You're kidding,' said Joey to Ernst. 'Iron bars and bayonets. You'll never get a Fourth Reich going with that sort of hardware.'

'You paid only for me,' said Ernst. 'My troops are here out of the goodness of their hearts. You want me to tell them to go home?'

'No, no, no,' said Joey. 'I'm sorry, iron bars and bayonets should do nicely.'

'OK, let's go,' said Ernst. '*Handa hock juden hunds.*'

Joey shot a corrosive look at Ernst. 'We aren't going in to stick the place up, ya fucking Nazi retard. Handa fucking hock indeed. Speak fucking English or you'll be getting a bit of old Sicilian right in the fucking head. No wonder you pricks lost the war. I mean, look at the way ya dressed. Doc Marten boots, jeans, an Adolf Hitler T-shirt and ya bloody granddad's old SS dress uniform jacket. We'll be lucky if the fucking Jews don't laugh 'emselves to death. Look at the way ya fucking mates are dressed. What, did they have a sale on flight jackets and Doc Martens at Vic Market?' he snarled.

Ernst looked down his nose at Joey. 'You stand there wearing red slip-on shoes and a green double-breasted sports jacket and dare to make adverse statements about me and my men. In my grandfather's day people like you were told to hit the showers and don't take ya fucking towels,' he said.

'What did you say to me, you big German dog?'

'Dog!' yelled Ernst. 'No one calls me a dog.'

'Did ya hear that?' exclaimed Jasmyn. The music and conversation in the club was pretty loud, but Niko had heard it too.

'Yeah, what the hell was that?' said Niko.

'Sounded like a car backfiring.'

Mark Dardo opened the door of the club and looked out into the dark, then closed the door quickly.

'What's up?' asked Micky Kelly.

Bronco Billy went and looked out a window into the dark outside. 'Fucking bunch of skinheads in some big fight,' he grunted.

Mark Dardo opened the door and walked out on to the footpath followed by Niko Ceka, Bronco Billy, Micky Kelly and Maltese Dave, then Jasmyn and assorted other patrons of the Albanian Club, namely various Albanian mental cases, Maltese criminals and Aussie gunnies from Collingwood.

The footpath in front of the club began to fill up, and no wonder. There was the most amazing sight: a handful of Sicilian gangsters led by Aussie Joe Gravano and a dozen neo-Nazis led by Ernst Kaltenbrunner punching the living guts out of each other. One Sicilian was lying in the street, shot, and one Nazi skinhead appeared to be down and out. Kaltenbrunner was using his handgun to pistol-whip all comers. They were cutting each other to shreds with iron bars, bayonets, knives and pistol butts. Then it got more willing. Gravano shot a skinhead and Ernst Kaltenbrunner returned fire and shot one more Sicilian.

'This is worth its weight in gold,' said Micky Kelly.

If there was one thing Albanians and Maltese both hated more than Italians, it was Germans. This insane display was priceless.

It got too much for Bronco Billy to resist. He yelled out and ran into the fight, screaming and throwing punches – and, bang, Kaltenbrunner shot him stone dead. Then Joey Gravano broke free and fired into the crowd on the footpath and one of the Maltese fell wounded, then Micky Kelly fired two shots in return and two skinheads fell. Mark Dardo and Niko Ceka started firing as Joey ran to his car. Another Sicilian and a skinhead dropped. It was pitch black as the Aussies, Albanians and Maltese moved in for the finish.

Gravano started his Chevy and took off as bullets shattered the rear window. Skinheads and one remaining Sicilian ran for their lives but Kaltenbrunner stood his ground, totally alone, apart from the dead and wounded around him.

Kaltenbrunner screamed, 'Come on, ya fucking dogs, come and get it,' and then fired two wild shots, hitting Micky Kelly in the stomach and wounding a Maltese.

Then a volley of return fire from more than a dozen handguns cut the German to bits. The big Nazi fell to his knees but refused to fall all the way, screaming blindly in German: '*Juden fucking dog Schwein!*'

Then Niko hit him in the head with a final shot and the Nazi fell backwards, deader than vaudeville.

Jasmyn held the badly wounded Micky Kelly in her arms. Mark Dardo took charge. 'Right,' he yelled. 'Jasmyn, Dave, get Micky to hospital, tell 'em he got shot in Allandale Road, St Albans.'

'What about Fremont Parade, West Sunshine?' replied Jasmyn.

'Are you two masterminds fucking joking?' screamed Micky. 'I mean does it matter, does it really fucking matter? Just get me to hospital. I know the bloody drill. Holy shit!'

'Sorry, Micky,' replied Mark.

Jasmyn and Maltese Dave loaded Micky into the back of a Fairmont and drove off. Mark turned to Niko, and the rest of the men gathered.

'OK, let's get this shit cleaned up. Shoot the fucking wounded and dump all the bodies in the back of Dave's panel van and we will bury these dogs. We can't have all this mess in front of the club.'

Niko put the barrel of his gun to the head of a wounded Maltese and pulled the trigger.

'Hey, Niko,' yelled Mark.

Niko looked up. 'Yes, brother,' replied Niko.

'Ahh, *their* wounded, mate,' said Mark carefully. 'Not ours.'

'Oh, sorry,' said Niko.

The rest of them stood in dumbfounded silence and looked at Niko in disbelief.

Niko flushed red with embarrassment at his breach of etiquette. He looked around into the faces of the men gathered and feebly repeated himself. 'I'm sorry, fellas,' he mumbled. It would be the last time he'd forget that in polite company you don't shoot your own wounded.

Later that morning, Benny Shapiro took a phone call at the house in Avoca Street, South Yarra, where Simone Tao had been an unwilling guest. Benny listened in silence for several minutes, then hung up and turned to Marven. 'If ya fucking read this in a Chopper book, ya wouldn't believe it,' he snorted.

'What?' asked Marven.

'Bronco Billy's dead, which is no great loss. And Micky Kelly is in the Footscray Hospital getting a bullet pulled out of his guts, so it was a good night out at the Albanian Club,' laughed Benny. 'You'd need a fucking corpse juggler to count the fucking bodies. They killed the big Nazi. Ha ha.'

'Good one.'

'Mark wants us to bring the Chinese moll over to Footscray.'

Marven looked at Benny, and Benny hung his head.

'And so you should hang your head too,' scolded Marven. 'She had important information. I leave you alone for 15 minutes to go to the shops and I come back to a dead chow hanging in the fucking bathroom.'

'She committed suicide,' said Benny defensively.

'I'm not saying she didn't hang herself,' said Marven, 'but only after you did your hands-on trick. Anyway, why did you leave her alone in the bathroom so she got a chance to top herself?'

Benny jumped in. 'Because I wanted to give her a bit of privacy while she had a shower.'

'Well, you weren't too fucking worried about privacy when

you were raping her five minutes after we got her through the front door,' retorted Marven.

'I'm sorry,' said Benny.

'Yeah, well, we will leave out the perverted details and just tell the boys she hung herself when our backs were turned,' said Marven. 'OK.'

'We could turn this into a plus,' said Benny hopefully.

'How?' asked Marven.

'Cut her head off and send it to the dagos,' said Benny. 'They aren't to know she committed suicide.'

Marven walked into the bathroom and inspected the naked body dangling from the shower rose with pantyhose. He was thinking aloud.

'Hmm, psychologically that could be a tactical winner. Yes, indeed, I know Micky Kelly would love that idea. OK, Benny, get her down and cut her head off.'

'Why me?' complained Benny.

'You're the one who fucked her. You're the one who left her alone in a locked bathroom and you're the one who brought up the wonderful idea of cutting her head off,' said Marven. 'So fucking cut it off and stop whinging. Bloody hell, Benny, get with the fucking programme and we haven't got all day, either, I promised to take Mother to the casino this afternoon, so get with it, OK?'

Melbourne, February 1998. Acting Detective Inspector Barry Mann sat in the bar of Barassi's Hotel in Bridge Road, Richmond, nursing a seven-ounce glass of scotch.

Big Barry was not a happy man. Beside him sat his mate Detective Senior Sergeant 'Big Jim' Reeves with an even larger glass of whisky in front of him. There was music coming from somewhere behind the bar, the melancholy sound of Hank Snow singing 'My Blue River Rose'.

'It's not fair,' complained Big Barry in disgust. 'It's just not fair. The bloody drug squad.'

'But they did promote ya,' said Big Jim.

'Yeah, promoted and demoted all at the same time. One minute I'm a humble shit kicker in the armed robbery squad. The next I'm an acting big deal shit kicker in the poxy drug squad.'

'The drug squad is not too bad,' said Big Jim. 'It could have been worse. They could have bunged ya into the vice squad.'

Barry Mann groaned. 'Yeah, I suppose every toilet has a silver lining. But I don't understand it, a fucking complaint against me made by that dog Guglameno, a complaint backed up by his dog mates Giordano and Monnella and fucking Capone, and the fucking ESD boot me up and out.'

'Jesus, mate,' said Jim Reeves, 'you're an acting inspector. You should be pleased.'

'Charlie and all the boys and you are still in the armed robbers. Why did I get the shaft?' asked Barry.

'Well, someone had to wear it and they pulled your name out of the hat,' said Reeves.

'I'm gonna dead-set fix them fucking dagos,' said Barry Mann. 'Believe me.'

'I got a better idea,' said Jim Reeves, and handed him a slip of paper.

Barry opened and read it. It had Aussie Joe Gravano's name and his Domain Road address on it. Then the words Sicilian Controller, Melbourne, Calabrian heroin connection, Aspanu clan, Sicily. Then there was a list of file numbers – state, federal and Interpol. And the entry codes for each.

Big Barry Mann put the paper in his pocket. 'Who give ya this?' he asked.

'Charlie Ford,' replied Jim Reeves.

'Would Charlie like a quick arrest?' asked Barry.

Big Jim mumbled something.

'What did you say?' asked Barry.

'I said,' answered Jim Reeves, 'that I don't think a fucking quick arrest was what Charlie and the crew had in mind.'

Big Barry Mann beamed a wide smile. 'Ha ha ha, so we're back in the saddle again, hey, Jim?'

Big Jim Reeves gave a sly smile. 'Charlie and the boys reckon having you in the drug squad might turn out to be not such a bad idea after all, Bazza. Ha ha.'

Big Barry Mann raised his glass.

'To Cowboy Westlock and Doc Holliday,' he said solemnly.

Big Jim Reeves raised his glass. 'Legends never die, Bazza. Legends never die. Ha ha.'

Mann looked a lot happier. 'Ya know, Jim, I was just thinking I might like the drug squad after all,' he chuckled.

CHAPTER 13

SOUTH OF THE BORDER

Melbourne, March 1998. Gaja Jankoo sat quietly in the Earl of Lincoln Hotel in Church Street, Richmond, drinking vodka and lemonade and waiting for her uncles Jonas and Jouzas, otherwise known as Johnny and Joe.

They walked in. 'Little Gaja,' said Uncle Johnny, and slapped her on the bottom.

'Your jeans too tight,' said Uncle Joe. 'Your bum on show.'

Gaja flushed. She was dressed a bit on the sexy side to be meeting her uncles. The jeans were old, torn and faded and so tight they fitted like a second skin, and the T-shirt was a punky number that did little to contain her tits. The joggers were acceptable but the earrings in both ears and the nostril and left eyebrow made her uncles look at her strangely. They ordered a Bundaburg rum each.

Johnny said, 'You look like a whore, little Gaja.'

'*Ake shik e bonka*,' replied Gaja, which, translated, meant she was telling him to go shit in a bottle – a common and comic Lithuanian insult.

Johnny Jankoo laughed. 'I didn't say you was a whore,' he said soothingly. 'I just meant you're dressed a bit slutty, that's all.'

'Yeah,' said Gaja, 'but don't worry about that. What about cousin Viko?'

They nodded. The death of Viko Radavic had to be avenged.

'I've done some checking with a friend of a friend over in Collingwood. Cassie Connor reckons it was the Albanians, Mark Dardo and Niko Ceka. Cassie tried to tell me it was Joey Gravano's fault because he was behind the death of Russian Frankie Lepetikha and cousin Viko killed Lepetikha for him. But cousin Viko was working for Gravano as a bodyguard on the night he was shot and Gravano got a bullet into Ceka after he shot Viko, so I don't see how anyone can blame Gravano.'

Johnny Jankoo said something in Lithuanian, which, translated, meant 'I'll cut his head off.'

'So it is Ceka and Dardo,' said Johnny.

'Albanians,' said Joe. 'We best be sneaky about this. Uncle Vlad won't like for us to start big war with fucking Albanians.'

'This isn't a war,' said Gaja, 'it is family personal private honour, revenge for the loss of a family member. It's our business.'

Johnny and Joe nodded.

'OK, we will fix Dardo and Ceka. But Gaja,' said Johnny, 'next time we meet wear proper lady's dress and pull all the shit off your face. You look like a side-show slut, fucking ridiculous.'

'Uncle Jonas,' said Gaja to Johnny, 'I love you but ya can bash ya fashion tips up ya arse.'

Joe laughed. 'I like the jeans and T-shirt,' he said.

Gaja turned to her Uncle Joe. 'Oh that's nice, Uncle Jouzas. So I'll just tell my father that his brother fancies me, will I?'

As Johnny and Joe left the hotel, Joe said to his brother, 'Young Gaja got no sense of humour, Johnny. None at all.'

'I blame Australia,' grumbled Johnny. 'Good girls all turn to bad girls in this country.'

Sicily, 1998. In a bar next to the airport, the Don's bodyguards Franco Di Tommaso and Luigi Monza sat drinking grappa and waiting for Joey Gravano's flight from Rome.

'If it wasn't for bad luck,' said Franco, 'fucking Aussie Joe would have no fucking luck at all.'

Luigi Monza nodded. 'Yes, Joey has done wonders in international cities all over the world but in Melbourne everything he touches turns to shit.'

'Yeah,' said Di Tommaso slyly, 'nothing cuts a man down to size more than returning to the old home town. Don Hector was born in Monreale but you notice he don't live there and he don't like to visit much, either.'

'Yes, I know what you mean,' replied Monza. 'Melbourne has become for us what Ireland became a long time ago,' said Franco.

'How do you mean?' asked Luigi.

'There is no mafia family, clan or operation in Ireland,' said Franco. 'England, yes. Even Scotland. But we gave Ireland back to the mad dog Irish a long time ago.'

Monza seemed surprised. 'I didn't know we had no interest in Ireland. We sell them guns, don't we?'

'Yeah,' said Franco, 'through America. We supply American-Irish and it goes on from there. But how can you operate a business in a land where on any Saturday night somebody might put a gun at your head and ask you what religion you are, then shoot you?'

Monza thought about this in silence, then he said, 'But the heroin trade in Ireland, we are behind it.'

'Yes,' said Franco. 'We supply a few local crews, but we have no Sicilians on the ground. It's a bit like Melbourne. We leave it all to Calabrians there: we pull the strings, while they get shot at. I think sooner or later Melbourne will end up a no-go zone. Even the Asian gangs who've spread all over the world mind their manners in Melbourne. The old-time Australian crooks are too hot to be stood over.'

'No wonder the rest of Australia call Melbourne Mexico. It's hot there, and I don't mean the weather. If Joey can't convince the Don that he can sort this shit out, the Don will pull him out and bring him back to Sicily. Joey's a good money mover, and he carries out orders.'

'Also,' continued Franco, 'the Don wasn't too fucking pleased about the Chinese lady's head being tossed through the front window of the Sicilian Soccer Club in Carlton. Joey has no true idea of how much money the death of the China doll cost the Don.'

'Drink up,' said Monza, 'his plane is coming in.'

Melbourne. Tommy Monnella, Al Guglameno and a few others sat in the back of the Regio Calabria Club in West Brunswick playing manila with Micky Mazzara and Bongo Bonventre.

'I'm telling ya, Al, it's none of our shit. Let fucking Gravano sort out his own shit,' said Monnella.

'Personally, I don't like the Sicilian snake and if the fucking Jews blow his wife up, I don't care. And if their Chinese whore accountant gets her fucking head cut off I care even less, and if every Albanian in Melbourne goes to war with every Sicilian I care even less again.'

Al Guglameno nodded, then spoke. 'Ya know, Tommy. If ya keep walking back and forth across a busy street, sooner or later ya gonna get hit.'

Tommy agreed, but thought to himself that, if you held a policeman's hand while crossing back and forth, you might not get hit. Al's good luck with the Melbourne police and legal system was the worst-kept secret in town. Everyone knew it, but no one dared speak of it.

Tommy bit his lip and looked down at his cards. He was still thinking. All Gravano's enemies got killed, and all Guglameno's got arrested. Ya wouldn't need to be a genius to figure it out, but, if the men under Guglameno suspected, then the Sicilians above him must certainly suspect. And, when Sicilians suspect a man, they kill him just to be on the safe side – unless they have a reason.

Tommy tossed his hand in. 'That's it, I've had enough. I'm going home.'

It was 6.30 in the morning. They'd been playing cards all night.

'OK,' said Big Al. 'I'll see ya tonight, Lygon Street. Then we'll hit that joint in King Street with a few of the boys.'

'Yeah, OK,' said Tommy, 'see ya later, mate. I'm going home. OK.'

'Yeah,' said Al. 'See ya, Tommy.'

As Monnella walked outside he checked the empty street, then walked towards his 1969 Chevy Corvette. Johnny Kingston had just sold it to him for $17,000, a dead-set steal. As he got into the car he could hear a faint whistling sound. Then the street exploded into a ball of flame. Tommy Monnella and his Corvette erupted in a fireball that rose 30 feet into the air, sending fragments through solid brickwork like a thousand full metal jacket bullets. It was as if the car had been hit with a flying bomb and the explosion was heard for a mile in every direction. What was left of Tommy Monnella was all over the neighbourhood, and looked like bolognese sauce.

Benny looked at Marven as he stood with the big Carl Gustov anti-tank gun. 'I think my arm and my collarbone is broken,' complained Marven.

'You're not meant to hold it. You're meant to mount it and fire it,' said Benny as he took the weapon from Marven.

'Yes,' said Marven, 'my left arm, my collarbone and, I think, some ribs are definitely broken.'

Mad Benny helped Marven to his car and put the anti-tank gun in the boot.

'Well, now I get to drive your car,' smiled Benny.

'Get me to hospital,' said Marven.

'Well,' said Benny, 'we could have used a landmine but, oh, no. You were hell-bent on using a fucking anti-tank gun. Let this be a lesson to you. Hacker said you had to mount it. You're lucky to be alive yourself.' Benny was rather enjoying Marven's embarrassing predicament. 'In future we will stick to the landmines. Agreed?'

'OK,' said Marven, 'just get me to fucking hospital.'

Sicily. When Joey Gravano got off the plane at Punta Raisi Airport he was surprised when Di Tommaso and Monza were there to greet him, as it was generally a job for the Benozzo brothers. Joey was a high-ranking member of the Aspanu clan and if not met by the Don himself it was good manners to be met by his uncle's personal bodyguards. It meant either of two things: Di Tommaso and Monza were climbing the clan ladder or Joey was slipping down it. This thought danced in Joey's head as he was shown to a bashed-up old 1955 model Ford Thunderbird. So the Don hadn't even sent his own car to collect Joey. No need to guess any more: Uncle Hector was pissed off.

Joey sat in the back of the car and relaxed. It was no use worrying. It was futile to try to escape punishment or death in Sicily. You could ask for a second chance or you could negotiate, but what would be would be. The hardest thing to run away from is the thing you fear most. Joey didn't fear death and in Sicily a man lived longer by going to meet death and making a deal with it.

Joey knew as the old car drove along that he was on his way either to die or to be given an ultimatum: fix the Melbourne fuck-up or else. One way or the other, Joey knew that Melbourne had turned into a stone in his uncle's shoe. Pietro Baldassare had been blown away at Tullamarine Airport with Joey standing two feet away. Joey hadn't even been able to protect his own wife in Melbourne. And he knew that the business with Simone Tao's head was the last straw. After all, Joey had introduced her to the clan, and now there were millions of dollars locked in accounts all over the world, and the only person who could unlock these accounts was the now headless Simone Tao. Yes, Joey was in trouble.

Monza spun the big car left, off the coast road.

'Where we going?' asked Joey.

Franco turned his head. 'Relaxio, Joey. Take it easy. The Don is at Montelepre.'

Joey sat back but his brain was speeding. Montelepre La Casa Di Lupare Bianca, the house of the white shotgun. Yes, thought Joey, he was in trouble all right. Only formal clan business took place there. Jesus, thought Joey, had it come to this? Surely he was entitled to one more chance. He was the victim of bad luck – not of high treason or foul treachery, for God's sake.

The house was surrounded by a high whitewashed stone wall. Behind the well-guarded gate was a small sunlit courtyard. The only shade was from a giant lemon tree that had grown up through the solid stone floor. In its shade was a table and six chairs. And at the table the old Don sat, smoking a big cigar and drinking grappa. In front of him sat a bowl of black olives and a plate of fried sliced salami. Next to him sat the Benozzo brothers, nursing double-barrel shotguns. A charming domestic scene, mafia style.

Joey was patted down for a weapon. This was more a routine than anything, as he'd just got off the plane, and was hardly likely to have been given anything by the pair who had met him. Still, in Sicily it paid to take no chances, and the Don's personal helpers didn't take any.

Joey greeted his uncle warmly in Sicilian.

The old man nodded. 'Sit down, nephew,' said the Don. 'Relaxio, Joey. Grappa?'

Joey nodded and took a glass of the homemade wine.

'So tell me, nephew. Are you just a fucking stupido or are you trying to destroy us all?'

'Please, Uncle,' said Joey.

'Don't fucking uncle me,' said the Don. 'The graveyards of Sicily are full of my nephews, grandchildren, not to mention half my sons. But they died for their treachery. I've never as yet had a relative killed for being an idiot. Now tell me, nephew, why should you live. Come on, give me a reason.'

The international escort service provided top-of-the-range

female companionship to gentlemen all over the world. It had branches in every big city. If a client had enough cash, he could order up what he liked and within 24 hours some walking wet dream could be either delivered almost anywhere. If the client was living in a tent in some Arabian desert and had a mobile phone and an American Express Gold Card the service would be able to provide a 24-carat-gold whore. It was organised, professional business and the ladies earned big money for themselves and a fortune for the firm.

Miss Donna Allan had spent a wonderful month in Thailand as the guest of a group of lovely Russian gentlemen involved in the heroin and arms industry. Mr Vladimir Zijit and Mr Grigor Zijit, two nice Russian brothers, and a dozen or so of their business colleagues, had kept Donna entertained for 30 days and nights. Then they had put her on a plane to Melbourne.

Donna had given away all pretence of being an air hostess and resigned from British Airways to take up what she loved most, full-time. She lived for excitement and loved the company of violent and dangerous men. She liked to be treated in a cavalier fashion sexually at the hands of a clientele that demanded discretion and secrecy. A clientele as sexually and as morally perverse as Donna herself.

She sat her shapely arse in her first-class seat and wiggled her hips about. No, there was no great discomfort. This was surprising, as one of her new Russian friends had, with the help of a little lubrication, inserted a plastic container about ten inches in length up her bottom. When her Russian friends had asked if she would be good enough to accommodate them in this matter, Donna had been more than happy to help out.

The plastic tube was watertight and hollow and contained 12 ounces of pure China white heroin. It was a sample her Russian friends wanted delivered to their friends in Melbourne. Donna had a phone number to ring, just in case, but was told that Mr Mark Dardo and Mr Niko Ceka would meet her at Tullamarine Airport. The arrangement was that Donna would remove the tube in the ladies room after take-off and replace it before landing. Donna required no payment for this. If a girl couldn't help her friends, it was a sad world indeed.

The Russians had told her that the Albanians she was to make contact with in Melbourne may want to employ her for the full 30 days before she had to return to London for other business commitments. Evidently the Albanians would be her cup of tea: that is, they were animals.

Donna looked at the little Japanese businessman sitting next to her as the plane took off. She loved her visits to Japan. The Japanese treated the sexual domination and mistreatment of women as normal and loved to degrade and dominate a white woman. The only trouble was, thought Donna, the Japs had pricks the size of a girl's little finger. A lady could accommodate 30 Japanese in a night and not even notice it. No wonder they hated women so much.

Donna crossed her long legs and the Japanese businessman took note as her dress crept up. Donna smiled a big, inviting smile then got out of her seat and reached to get her carry bag. The dress rode higher. She would just pop along to the ladies and remove what needed to be removed then return to attend to the little Japanese.

By the time she got to Melbourne she'd have this little bonsai businessman lighter by several thousand or her name wasn't Donna Allan.

Joey Gravano flew out of Sicily with the Don's words ringing in his ears. Micky Kelly, Marven Mendelsohn, Benny Shapiro, Mark Dardo and Niko Ceka … kill 'em all, or put the barrel of your gun in your own mouth and pull the trigger.

The death of Simone Tao was a financial nightmare but it served the Don right, as the old man said himself, for placing his faith and his money in the new technology. Imagining that a fortune in Aspanu money could all be kept safe and secure on some floppy disk in the hands of some floppy Chinese whore was as much the Don's fault as Joey's. The truth was, old Hector had liked the Chinese girl and trusted her and she had not betrayed the Aspanu clan. She had simply got herself kidnapped while under Joey's protection and had her head cut off, and with her vanished the whereabouts of 30 fucking million dollars. Or was it 40 million?

Don Hector didn't know how to operate a microwave oven, let alone a computer. The whole thing was a high-tech nightmare. But, said the Don, it was a fuck-up he too had to share in. Joey had made the introduction but Simone had swept the old Don off his feet, so too much was placed in her care. It was the Don taking part of the blame that saved Joey's life this time, but there must not be any more mistakes.

Joey's plane left Italy at about the same time that Donna Allan landed at Tullamarine and, sure enough, Mark Dardo and Niko Ceka were there to meet her. Niko noticed her first and nudged Mark Dardo.

Mark nodded towards Donna. 'Miss Allan?' he said.

'Oh, yes,' said Donna.

'My name is Mark Dardo. This is my cousin Niko Ceka. Do you have any luggage?' asked Mark.

'No, none. Only my carry bag,' replied Donna, indicating the small leather bag she held in her left hand.

Mark looked down at the bag in a sort of puzzled horror and Donna laughed.

'Oh, no, Mr Dardo. It's not in there, it's in a safer place than that,' she said and gave a little wiggle of her hips. 'I've a letter to give you from Mr Zijit. That is, Mr Vladimir Zijit.'

She pulled an envelope out of her jacket pocket and handed it to Mark. It was written in Albanian and Mark read it in front of Niko and Donna.

'What does it say, brother?' asked Niko.

'It says,' said Mark, 'this letter will introduce Miss Donna Allan who is a personal and good friend of the Zijit brothers and that they vouch for her honesty and character. It also says –' Mark looked at Donna and she smiled '– that she loves it two at a time, and will accommodate any number of men in a night if requested. If she misbehaves or protests or whimpers or makes any complaints whatsoever, she is to be beaten to within an inch of her life like a disobedient slut.'

The letter went on: 'Mark, she is the craziest, twisted bitch, pain freak whore I've ever come across. Try not to kill her. All the best, Vlad.'

Mark and Niko looked at Donna in amazement, and she smiled at them both.

'Well,' said Mark, 'that is quite a letter of introduction, Miss Allan. I don't know what to say.'

'I do,' said Niko. 'Let's get out of here and try her on for size.'

Donna was marched from the airport to a waiting car and driven to a nearby motel. While having a shower she removed the tube, cleaned it and handed it to Mark – only to be joined in the shower by a naked Niko. Mark pulled the shower curtain back and said, 'Hold out your arm.'

'I don't use heroin,' said Donna.

Niko grabbed her arm and held it out and snarled, 'Stay still. Don't worry. I've only used half a match head, a very small amount. You won't die.'

Mark hit the vein, jacked the fit back then plunged it in. Within moments the smack hit and she said, 'Ohhhh yeah,' then she vomited in the shower and washed her face under the water.

'Good?' asked Mark.

Donna nodded with a drugged smile, her eyes half-closed. She moaned, lurched forward and vomited again, then hung her head under the hot water of the shower. She felt wrapped in a cloud of cotton wool. So much for testing the quality of the Russian's heroin.

When Niko blew his load she didn't even feel it. Mark replaced Niko in the shower and got into the act. She wasn't fully aware of the changing of the guard until Mark slapped her across the face. There was no pain, but she loved it anyway. Force of habit.

Donna remembered being taken from the shower and put in the large motel bed, where she was subjected to lots of Albanian, from every angle. When she awoke in the morning Mark gave her another small shot of the magic powder, and she showered and dressed and hopped in the back of their car and was driven to the Albanian Club in Yarraville. The Russians were quite right, she decided, the Albanians were animals.

Donna had her money, credit cards, passport, carry bag and clothing taken and was allowed to keep only her high heels and high-cut panties. Her bra was taken from her and she was told to get up on the bar and dance.

She protested that she wasn't a good dancer and received a beating that went far beyond her sick sexual masochistic fantasies. For once, she was in true pain and fear. She was then ordered into a shower and told to wash the blood off. Her nose was broken. She was supplied with a new set of high heels and a new set of high-cut knickers, and felt no pain after another taste of heroin.

It was decided that a girl with a bashed-up face could hardly be used as a dancer at the club so Donna was locked in a rear room that contained a double bed and an adjoining toilet and shower. For some reason Donna recalled the Australian mafia guy in New York telling her she belonged in a lock shop brothel. Sure enough, the door opened and men entered two at a time and Donna serviced them all until she lost count. Any failure to show full interest in her work was greeted with a vicious slapping about the face.

In the morning she got a heroin needle and a shower and she was allowed to rest in the painless cloud of peace the needle brought her. She knew that the night would bring a full repeat of the night she had just endured, but she also knew that her new Albanian masters would provide her with another needle full of heaven beforehand. She didn't care, and closed her eyes. She had at last reached the pits of hell. She had been tempting fate for a long time, and now it had happened. She had fallen all the way to the bottom. But she was such a sick pup that it was what part of her had been looking for.

The trouble was, at the minute, too many Albanian heavies were looking for that part of her, too. She'd gone from a high-class $1000-an-hour call girl to being tossed to the dogs for $50 a pop. And it could only get worse.

She should have listened to her mother, after all.

CHAPTER 12

RIGHT WHACK

What you lose on the roundabout you pick up
on the swings and slides.

April 1998. Micky Kelly walked out of Footscray Hospital with a long, leggy girl with blonde hair tied up in a top knot. She was wearing a skintight all-black outfit that clung tight to every curve, except for a baggy black T-shirt. Under the T-shirt she had a Colt .32 automatic handgun tucked tight under a wraparound velcro tummy belt. The beauty of such a girl carrying a firearm was that men noticed only her hips and arse and hair and her pouty face hidden behind dark glasses. They couldn't help it. The little head always ruled the big head.

As Jasmyn escorted Micky from hospital, even the police

who were watching the pair didn't think for a moment that the cheeky-looking blonde might be carrying a loaded gun.

Maltese Dave opened the door of the Ford LTD and Micky got in the passenger's seat. Dave got behind the wheel and Jasmyn got in the back behind Micky. The two were on Micky's payroll – Maltese Dave as driver, and Jasmyn as bodyguard. She carried the gun and was quite willing to use it. Maltese Dave also carried a gun, a .32-calibre Young revolver, and Micky had a Heckler and Koch automatic in the glovebox.

No one expects a man's exotic dancer companion to pull out a shooter and blast away at the first sign of trouble. Having Jasmyn on hand and armed up was a sneak go the enemy would not look for. They would concentrate all fire power on Micky and Dave, allowing Jasmyn vital seconds to return fire.

She had spent a week practising, and could hit six out of six beer bottles at 30 yards. She had the Colt loaded and carried an extra clip with six rounds. Jasmyn liked her new role. As a club dancer she was treated as a dumb blonde, but now the men around Micky Kelly treated her with newfound respect. Funny what a pistol can do.

She had shown courage under fire at the shoot-out outside the Albanian Club and Micky did not forget whose arms held him after he had been shot. The only problem was that Jasmyn was Dave's girl and it would be putting a hole in his manners for Micky to try to get into her pants. But Micky copped it. You can't have it all your own way all the time, he thought.

As Maltese Dave drove Micky towards Squizzy Taylor's

Hotel in Gertrude Street, Fitzroy, Mark Dardo and Niko Ceka were pulling up in front of that very establishment. With them was a beautiful redhead wearing sunglasses and a tight T-shirt. A close look at the sexy face revealed the lady had a broken nose, but this slight facial flaw only added to the raw sex appeal. Like Jasmyn, the lady with the two Albanians also had her hair up in a top knot.

Donna Allan was now well and truly Albanian property. She had a raging heroin habit that the Albanians fed. She relied on them for food and drink, pocket money, clothing and make-up. She had to ask them and they would provide. She followed her Albanian masters around like a puppy. She acted on any instruction of a sexual nature with blind obedience. She was in a world she could not escape and the gates that held her were made of heroin.

She was serving a life sentence – but not a long one. It would last only as long as her physical beauty held out. Her sexual charms kept her alive, but the drugs and daily sexual abuse would age her by 20 years in about two, then she would either die of an overdose – which would be a kindness – or allowed to wander and beg like a starving dog for money or drugs from men who no longer wanted to buy the worn-out goods she had. That route, too, was a shortcut to a pauper's grave. Heroin is a heavenly highway, but it leads to hell.

In Melbourne, as in Ireland, Murphy's Law and the criminal law are two and the same. So, when Micky Kelly, Maltese Dave and the lovely Jasmyn walked through the door of Squizzy Taylor's Hotel to be greeted with wild hellos and hugs and kisses all around from Mark Dardo, Niko Ceka and Donna Allan, it set the scene for farce.

Johnny and Joe Jankoo, the Lithuanian brothers on the hunt for the Albanians, and Joey Gravano, on the hunt for Micky Kelly and the Albanians, pulled up in front of the hotel at the same time and unbeknown to each other. The Lithuanians parked on one side of Gertrude Street, Aussie Joe Gravano on the other. Both Gravano and the Jankoos intended shedding blood. Like the Irish bank robber who ran into the bank only to have his gun taken from him by the three men already robbing the bank, the Jankoo brothers walked through the front door of the hotel at about the same time as Joey was about to cross the street. As Gravano looked to the left, then to the right, and to the left again, checking traffic, he heard gunfire. Three shots, then three more. Joey could tell from the sound that different guns were being used.

Joey was frozen to the spot. He reached under his coat for his .45 Gold Cup automatic and watched the door as Micky Kelly came out, carrying a handgun, followed by Maltese Dave, also holding a shooter. Then came a long leggy blonde, also carrying a rod. Then he saw (and heard) a redhead chick screaming. As Joey pulled out his shooter and aimed it at Micky Kelly, he was a fraction distracted by the thought that he had seen or met the redhead before.

Joey snapped off six shots at Micky Kelly. The blonde girl took aim at him and returned three quick rounds, but the slugs hit passing cars. Joey ducked and ran back to his car and started the motor just as a fourth slug shattered the driver's side window. His right eye filled with blood as he sped away. Maltese Dave put two shots through his rear window, but it was all too late. Of the six shots fired in Micky Kelly's direction one hit the red-haired whore in the throat, and she lay dying on the footpath. Two other shots caught Micky in the chest. He was mortally wounded. Jasmyn tried to pick up the dying Kelly and Maltese Dave yelled, 'Leave him, Jas, he's finished.'

Micky Kelly looked up into the eyes of the crying girl and said, 'Go on, Princess, piss off.'

Jasmyn was dragged, crying, back to the car by Maltese Dave and driven away. Inside the hotel bar lay the dead bodies of Mark Dardo, Niko Ceka and the Jankoo brothers. The Jankoo brothers had got off only three rounds, one into the head of Mark Dardo and two into the chest of Niko Ceka, before Jasmyn had punched three return rounds into them – two into Johnny Jankoo's chest and one into Joe's face. She had then replaced the clip – still holding three rounds – with the full clip, as she didn't want to hit the footpath outside the pub with only three shots left.

Maltese Dave didn't freeze up when the Lithuanians opened fire but he did react slowly because of the surprise, as did Micky Kelly and the Albanians. What amazed them was Jasmyn's lightning response. With hands as quick as light, she took up the devil's challenge and went into the night, thought Micky, as he lay dying on the footpath.

He turned his head to see the open eyes of the dead Donna looking straight at him. A crowd gathered around him and

Micky could hear the sound of the ambulance, or was it a police car?

Who's gonna tell my dad, thought Micky. Jesus, he's gonna be mad at me. Don't go getting yourself into any bloody trouble, son, he always says. Ha ha. Maybe Jasmyn and Dave would tell him. What the fuck were those mad Lithuanians doing? And Gravano? Did Jasmyn clip him with one of her shots?

As Micky lay dying, an old song came into his head and he mumbled the words. 'Oh ya can laugh and ya can cry, ya can bleed until ya die but one way or the other, son, ya gonna pay the bill.'

He laughed and coughed up blood.

Then it all went black except for a tunnel of white light. Micky felt at peace and warm and began to walk through the light, but to the onlookers staring down at him in front of Squizzy Taylor's Hotel he was going no place at all. He was dead.

Melbourne, June 1998. Benny Shapiro rang Marven Mendelsohn and invited him to come over to have a look at Benny's new car. Benny was a pest, but he was also the closest thing to a friend Marven had in the world, next to his mother. But Benny did give Marven the shits, as he had to humour Benny like a kid.

Marven kissed his mother and got into the 1954 Studebaker and drove quietly over to Benny's place in Beaconsfield Parade, St Kilda. As Marven drove along, he began to sing quietly to himself an old Christian hymn. As a rule, Jewish hitmen weren't big on hymns but, although he didn't know all the words, he did like the Mahalia Jackson tape his mother played at home after the evening meal. The Christian religion, while a total load of flapdoodle to Marven, was given to producing nice religious music, especially black American Baptist gospel singers. And, as Marven drove along, mulling over the trivial nonsense of religious music and Benny's new car, he began to sing. 'Just a closer walk with thee, granted Jesus let it be, nearer my God I am to thee, Oh let it be, dear Lord, let it be.'

As he pulled up outside Benny's place, he saw Benny standing on the footpath with a big smile on his dial.

'Come and have a look,' said Benny, practically jiggling up and down, like a small boy who's caught a frog, 'it's in the garage.'

Marven followed Benny to the garage and Benny pulled the roller door up. Inside was a bright-yellow Volvo with a surfboard on the roof rack and Tasmanian numberplates. It took Marven a moment to register, then he stared at Benny, who could hardly contain his laughter.

'Benny, this is in really serious bad taste,' he scolded. 'It would serve you right if you're arrested, or at least pulled up every day, if you drive that around.' He paused and added, 'Tell me that it's not bloody Martin Bryant's, is it?'

Marven looked hard at Benny, who was laughing so much he was nearly pissing himself. Then he turned on his heel and walked back to the Studebaker.

'Ya got no sense of humour, Marven,' yelled Benny.

Marven got into his car, opened the driver's side window and started the motor.

'If you want to cruise around town in a yellow Volvo with a surfboard on the roof rack, Ben, then ya on ya own,' he yelled. 'Ya fucking sick schmuck.'

Benny stopped laughing. 'It's only a bit of a giggle, Marven.'

'Yeah,' said Marven, 'and in a way I can see the comedy of it, but we have our necks on the chopping block. The Albanians are dead, at least the ones we do business with. Micky Kelly is dead. Our names are on the list and you're out buying fucking yellow Volvos like some psychopathic Monty Python. Ya wanna start getting serious, Ben. If we don't get them fucking dagos, they will get us. Jesus.'

Benny took the dressing down seriously. 'I'm sorry, Marv,' he muttered.

'Yeah, well, get with it.' Then Marven stopped and thought again. 'Is the Volvo registered in your name, Ben?'

'Yeah,' said Benny.

'Hmm, pity,' replied Marven.

'Ya got an idea, hey, Marv?' asked Benny, smiling at being let off the hook.

Marven gave a sly grin. 'Maybe, maybe. We'll see. OK, mate, see ya later.'

'Yeah,' said Benny, wondering what was going on in Matchstick Marven's marvellous mind. 'See ya, Marven.'

Aussie Joe Gravano didn't like to call on Al Guglameno and his crew but he needed a hand. Badly. Joey had two trustworthy Sicilians, Charlie Coppola and Elio Monza, but he needed a lot bigger crew to handle the storm that was cooking up.

Gravano needed Guglameno and his crew to help him handle the Jews. After all, the Jews had got Monnella, so the fucking Calabrians were honour-bound to get with the programme. Tony Capone and Eddie Giordano were both anxious to help Joey, but big Al – as always – was a fucking misery guts who dragged his feet on every issue. It was only Aussie Joey's mention of taking it all to Poppa Di Inzabella that prompted Al to suddenly appear with a smile on his face, the arsehole. Why Uncle Hector wanted to let this Calabrian dog live was a puzzle to Joey, but Joey was a soldier and didn't question orders.

His eye was getting better after having glass from the car window removed from it, but he still had to wear an eye patch that made him look more like a Sicilian pirate than ever. The Calabrians had taken to calling him Captain Pugwash behind his back.

When rumours of this reached Joey's ears, he laughed. But he asked himself how a pack of Calabrians from Lygon Street, Carlton, would be able to come up with a bit of classic Aussie comedy straight out of the television history books.

Hmm, he thought to himself. Too much time spent drinking with Aussie coppers. Sometimes people give themselves away without knowing it. The Calabrian Onorata Societa. What a joke.

Joey thought of Tina. If the mafia is so powerful why can't

it protect itself against madmen. Then Joey remembered the old proverb: 'no strength in swordsmanship, however just, can stand secure against a madman's thrust.'

Joey was thinking hard. Two Jews to kill, why should that be so hard?

The whole thing was a lie, and the shame of it made Joey sick. A man could only pretend so long before it started to eat him away. Joey was in a dangerous mood.

It was a wet night. The few people on the streets were running for any place that was dry. It was warm and cosy in the Calabrian Soccer Club in Cardigan Street, Carlton. Big Al Guglameno, Tony Capone, Eddie Giordano and members of each man's own personal crews were there.

Aussie Joe Gravano had just arrived with Charlie Coppola and Elio Monza. The personal and regional grudges between these men had been put aside. This night they were all Italian brothers against a common enemy, the Jews.

As the various crews in the club talked softly about battle plans to be put into action, Marven Mendelsohn sat a hundred yards up the road in his 1954 Studebaker. Beside him sat Maltese Dave.

'Stop playing with ya gun,' said Marven to Dave.

Dave said something in Maltese that sounded like a cat getting strangled, but meant 'Get fucked'.

'Where the hell is Benny and Jasmyn?' said Marven.

'Driving over here in a fucking yellow Volvo with a surfboard on top. They'll get pulled over for sure.'

'I got Cassie Connor driving the Al Shiek brothers over. They have a personal blue with Eddie Giordano.'

'Abdul and Ahmet?' said Dave. 'This is like the United Nations, Maltese, Aussies, Jews and fucking Arabs.'

'Yeah,' said Marven. 'And, I think, if I'm not mistaken, that V8 Commodore in front of us is the Kravaritis brothers. I think Cassie arranged that through Hacker Harris.'

'Jesus,' replied Dave, 'Albanians.'

A dark-blue 1977 Ford LTD pulled up in Cardigan Street alongside Marven. Cassie Connor wound the window down and so did the Al Shiek brothers. Marven did the same.

'*Salam alecam*,' said Abdul Al Shiek to Marven.

'*Alecam A Salam*,' replied Marven politely in his best Jewish Arabic.

Cassie seemed to find this multi-cultural stuff a touch annoying. 'Talk English,' she said. 'And you can bag ya fucking head as well,' she yelled at Dave. 'Micky Kelly got shot because the Maltese brought fucking knives to a bloody gunfight.'

'Take it easy,' said Marven. 'The enemy is in there,' he said, pointing to the Calabrian Soccer Club. 'Now, as soon as Mad Benny gets here with Jasmyn, we can rock and roll.'

Marven was talking tough, but he didn't feel too good about the events to come.

As Benny and Jasmyn pulled into Cardigan Street, Benny was waffling on, as always.

'The point is, Jas,' said Benny, 'Wing Commander Douglas

Bader, the World War II British fighter pilot who had two tin legs — well, he is famous, but how many people know the name of the surgeon who removed his legs?'

Jasmyn looked at Benny as if he had grown two green heads. 'Well, I don't reckon many people would, Benny,' she said.

'His name,' said Benny, with a superior smile, 'was Doctor or Mister Joyce.' He paused. 'I bet ya didn't know that.'

Jasmyn shook her head. He wasn't called Mad Benny for nothing.

Benny parked the yellow Volvo in front of the Calabrian Soccer Club, then jammed the horn on. It blasted out non-stop and Jasmyn and Benny jumped out of the car and ran down Cardigan Street into the dark.

Aussie Joe Gravano stepped out of the club into the rain with the army of Italians behind him to see what the racket was. When they saw the yellow Volvo with the surfboard on the roof rack and the horn blowing, the men around him laughed. But Joey thought of the Walsh Street set-up and the cat in the birdcage murder, and reached for his gun.

Suddenly, the night erupted into gunfire, and within moments the shooting started from three different directions. Joey dived to the footpath and hid behind a car as did Big Al Guglameno, but Charlie Coppola and Elio Monza, along with Tony Capone and Eddie Giordano, backed up by the small army of Italians, ran blindly into the rain and darkness firing handguns.

There was a scream. 'Eddie Akadahs! Eddie Abbi!' The voice

belonged to Terry the Turk, a half-Turkish, half-Italian hood who looked on Eddie Giordano as a father figure. Aussie Joe knew that Eddie Giordano must be dead. He crawled along the gutter, soaking wet, and hid under a car as the battle raged about him. There was screaming in half a dozen languages and more gunfire than Joey had ever heard before.

Big Al Guglameno got to his feet and ran blindly down Cardigan Street, leaving his men to fight while he escaped. Joey wanted to get out from under the car and fight, but in a panic situation a man reacts on the fight or flight impulse, and even brave men can flee in the face of madness.

Joey could think only of Tina. As he lay there in the dark under the car with the bullets and the blood and the groans and screams and the yellow Volvo's horn, he began to cry.

Sicily, late 1998. It seemed that Joey had vanished, and Don Hector was worried. His body hadn't been found with all the others outside the Calabrian Soccer Club in Melbourne after the shoot-out that had made world headlines. Uncle Hector didn't need to ask what happened: he saw it on TV, heard it on the radio, read about it in Italian newspapers. The two Jews got whacked all right, along with about a dozen others – Arabs, Albanians, Maltese, Italians, Turks, Greeks, Australians – in the yellow Volvo ambush, or the surfboard shoot-out, as various papers called it.

The whole thing was madness. Don Hector was making arrangements through Poppa Di Inzabella to withdraw all Sicilian control and, for a price, hand total control over to the

Calabrians. Let them oversee the madness. The Sicilians would remain financial shareholders and major investors and have a seat at the table, but Italian crime in Melbourne would now be the Calabrians' headache. Let them have it. The money wasn't worth the worry. Jesus Christ, thought Hector Aspanu, cats in birdcages, yellow Volvos with surfboards and tooting horns. It's like the devil's Disneyland.

The whole thing was like some comic nightmare – but where was Joey? A dozen dead, and another dozen still in hospital, but no Joey. An unfamiliar emotion hit the old Don. It was sadness. He realised he truly loved his stupid nephew, even though he did little to show it. He did not want Joey dead. He wanted him back. He would abuse him, of course, but he wanted him.

Don Hector sat quietly under the shade of the big lemon tree in the courtyard of the house of the white shotgun, drinking grappa and smoking a Cuban cigar.

The Benozzo brothers stood near by. Franco Di Tommaso and Luigi Monza came through the front gate with a third man.

'Don Hector,' said Di Tommaso as he introduced Carlo Saietta as 'a friend of ours from the Death Society of Rome'.

The Don looked at Saietta and said, 'The Saietta family and the Gravanos are related. Your family is related to the Aspanu clan, correct?'

'Yes, Don Hector,' said Carlo Saietta. 'But the society in Rome – well, we not too big on family, not like you Sicilians.'

Then he got down to business. 'We got your nephew. You can get angry and kill me, but let's get realistic. In a blood war, you'd lose. We start with the children first, and work up. You mafia Goombatas belong to the funny papers and the American movies. We want one million American or we send you Joey Gravano's ears. We will bury his body like a dead dog.'

Rage welled up inside the Don, then his old age hit him and he knew he belonged to the past, and he was talking to the future. Or, at least, it would be better to act that way if he wanted to see Joey alive.

Don Hector looked at his men. He could see they did not want to be ordered to kill this Roman renegade. The old world was standing face to face with the new and the old world felt too tired and too weak to fight it.

'A million American dollars, you say,' said the Don. 'That is very cheap.'

Carlo Saietta replied, 'A little here, a little there, it all adds up.'

'I know the game,' said the Don. 'A million is too small a price to squabble over. Di Tommaso, arrange the money for this bastardo bandieto,' said Don Hector, 'and get Joey back, OK?'

Di Tommaso looked stunned.

'Presto, presto, presto!' screamed Don Hector. 'Get my Joey back.'

As Di Tommaso and Monza left the courtyard with the Roman crook, the Don thought to himself, I'm dying. I'm an old man. Joey is my future, and he must take my place, then he can put all the wrongs to right. Jesus, whoever would have dreamed they would dare attack the Aspanu clan this way. And I surrendered and gave in like a girl. Jesus Christ.

Then the Don smiled. A million dollars? They could have demanded ten million and got it.

'Joey, come home to me?' said the Don, out loud. 'Please come home.'

Two days later in a Palermo restaurant, Aussie Joe Gravano sat with the Don and his men. He ordered a bottle of grappa and sliced raw steak with sauce.

'You're a fucking animal, Joey,' said Don Hector, then he looked at the waiter then down at the menu. 'I'm not hungry,' said the old man, then changed his mind and ordered octopus, scampi and grappa. The others ordered and the Don said to Joey, 'You're paying for this, you have cost me a fucking...'

Monza interrupted him to speak to the waiter.

'Shut up, I'm talking!' snapped the Don with some of his usual venom. 'You have cost me a million dollars,' said the Don to Joey, grumbling in a friendly way. The Don would never let him forget this. To be kidnapped by the ragamuffin shitpot Roman street bandits – the Sicilians had suffered a public relations disaster.

'Joey, Joey,' the Don muttered, 'for God's sake, what happened?'

Joey smiled. 'Shit like this don't happen in the movies, hey, Padrino?'

The Don smiled back. 'Maybe we should get Robert de Niro to take over, hey? Or that young one, what's his name?' he said.

'Tarantino,' said Joey. 'Quentin Tarantino.'

'Ha, ha,' laughed the Don. 'Yeah, we better ring Hollywood. They do it fucking better than we do.' 'Jesus, Joey,' said the Don, half serious. 'If it weren't for bad luck, mamma mia…'

'Yeah,' replied Joey, 'we'd have no fucking luck at all. Ha ha.'

CHAPTER 15

THE APPLE CUCUMBER

> *Woe unto you lawyers for ye have taken away*
> *the key of knowledge.*
> LUKE, 11:52

Melbourne, September 1998. Big Al Guglameno had soon recovered from the loss of face and manpower after the shoot-out. He regrouped with the help of Peter Trimboli, Paul Picassos, Charlie Gangitano, Micky Gall and a heap of other blokes with interesting names mostly of the Italian persuasion, including Jimmy Di Inzabella.

Big Al was now a full-blown Calabrian honoured society lieutenant, overseeing all its heroin operations in Melbourne. So it was interesting to see him sitting in Dan O'Connell's Hotel in Canning Street, Carlton, talking to Detective Senior

Sergeant 'Big Jim' Reeves from the armed robbery squad. Not that it would have greatly surprised anybody in the underworld, as the Calabrian mob flaunted its association with the Victoria police, and various members of the society could often be found in comic conversation with detectives. The lack of Sicilian watchdogs allowed such open displays of dubious conduct. The conversation at Dan O'Connell's proved that the Sicilians' instincts were pretty sharp.

'It's gotta be done, Al,' said Big Jim. 'And you're the only one who can pull it off.'

Big Al shook his head. 'The Sicilian hates my guts and I'm sure he knows I'm in with your blokes. He's never trusted me,' said Al. 'It won't work.'

'He might go along with it if you give him a good enough reason,' said Jim Reeves. 'Charlie Ford wants it and Barry Mann and his crew will do it, but you gotta set it up for us, OK?'

'Or what?' said Al Guglameno.

'Or,' hissed Jim Reeves, 'you'll pull a gun on some nice young policewoman one night and she will blow ya Calabrian dog head off. Got it, fat boy?'

Big Al sat in silence. 'When?' he said, after a long and pregnant pause.

'As soon as. Here's a phone number, ring me when ya got Joey with ya, or when ya gonna meet him next, OK? Just fucking do it.'

'Yeah, she's sweet,' said Al. 'Consider it done.'

As Jim Reeves walked out of the bar, Al Guglameno

thought, I'll set Joey up today and tomorrow the fucking cops will get someone to set me up. In the end no one wins but the fucking undertaker.

But Al knew he had no way out. The one who wins the game is the one who lives the longest. In the end, survival was all that mattered. He thought about the old saying: 'if you wanna be a spider then you gotta live in a web.'

Big Jim Reeves made a quick phone call to his boss, Charlie Ford of the armed robbery squad. The recent Ethical Standards Department investigations and the chief commissioner's clean up or get out policy had seen some amazing changes. Transfers, demotions, sackings, golden handshakes, 'don't come backs' and promotions. All in order to avoid a Royal Commission, naturally. No one, least of all the premier and the police minister, wanted to have questions asked that they didn't already know the answers to. Such things can lead to embarrassment.

A lot of colourful cops vanished into the police equivalent of the Bermuda Triangle. Detective Sergeant Susan Hilton remained in the armed robbery squad, as did Jim Reeves, and was promoted to boot. Charlie Ford was promoted and Sandra Emerson was promoted and transferred out of internal investigations and put in charge of Charlie Ford – the commissioner's idea of putting a softer face on the armed robbery squad.

Seven new boys were transferred out of the special operations group and sent to the armed robbers. Big Barry

Mann was promoted into the drug squad. But there were three strange appointments. They brought back three old hands to the armed robbers who had got the arse out to St Kilda, Collingwood and Fitzroy CIB years before for — to put it politely — excessive zeal. They were Dirty Larry Clark, Rocky Bob Porter and Crazy Ray Williams. And, somehow, Herb 'Hatter' Hannigan got transferred to the drug squad. He had the nickname because he was as mad as a hatter. He was 47 years of age and still a Detective Senior Constable. He'd shoot his own mother if she didn't put her hands up fast enough. He'd been booted out of the armed robbery squad back in the early 1980s for 'excessive use' of his police-issue revolver after discharging it three times into the air at a Collingwood–Carlton footy match at Victoria Park. That was his third offence. He had shot a bank robber two years previously — once to stop him and five more times to make sure — and another time he took pot shots at the wedding cake, blind drunk, after gatecrashing a federal policeman's wedding.

How Hatter Hannigan had remained in the police force and out of jail was magnificent. The new broom had raised a lot of dust and put a lot of bright new sparks in bright new places. But it had also swept some evil old spiders along with it.

The drug squad had become a pansy-boy yuppie joke. All polish, no punch, whereas the old armed robbery squad had been all punch, no polish. It was all just a case of rearranging the deckchairs on a ship that wasn't sinking. True, it was taking on a little water, but the good ship Victoria police didn't sink. It stayed afloat while police forces in other states broke up.

Why? Simple, really. In Melbourne, the police might punch a bullet into you for next to nothing but most of them won't take your money. They will shoot ya but they won't rob ya. Corruption is what sinks a police force. Shooting a criminal six times when a stern talking-to would be all he would have got in any other state – that's not corruption, that's just the way it works south of the border, down Mexico way.

You can hold a Royal Commission into police corruption, cash and drugs and prostitution, graft, bribery and so on but you can hardly hold a Royal Commission into the combined culture and mentality of an entire police force that sees itself as some sort of latter-day Texas Ranger outfit.

The cowboy mentality runs as deep in the Victoria police, as it does in the Victoria criminal. Mexico – whoever thought up that nickname for Melbourne and Victoria was spot on. But we digress.

Charlie Ford picked up the phone. 'Yeah. G'day, Jim. Yeah, yeah, good.'

Big Jim Reeves was trying to explain something in code over the phone. 'Bugger the KGB bullshit, Jim. Did the dago go for it, or what?'

'Yes,' replied Jim Reeves.

'Good,' said Charlie. 'Fuck the Sicilians, they wouldn't tell ya what day it is – but the Calabrians, well, ya can't shut the pricks up. Ha ha.'

He was in full stride now. 'Ya can't win the fucking drug war – and ya can tell Bazza I said this – but ya sure as hell can manage it. We'll let the Calabrians float as long as they help us. Sink everyone else, OK? Remind Bazza of the immortal words of Graeme Westlock, as long as the dogs keep barking, they can keep breathing. Ha ha. Gravano is off tap because we've got fucking Guglameno on tap, that's all there is to it.'

'How do we play it, boss?' asked Jim Reeves.

'The dago will use the cucumber routine, anyway,' said Charlie. 'I don't need to be involved no more. You work it all out with Bazza, OK, mate?'

'OK,' said Jim, and hung up.

The old apple cucumber trick, thought Charlie to himself. Well, that's something we can thank the old Collingwood crew for. Shiftiest trick ever invented. Roy Reeves, Micky Van Gogh and John McCall, they would have made handy coppers.

The apple cucumber relied on the friend of the target unknowingly leading the victim to his death, with the friend totally unaware he was being used as a goat to trap a lion.

Young Jimmy Di Inzabella had always looked up to Aussie Joe Gravano, and as the grandson of old Poppa Di Inzabella, Aussie Joe trusted Jimmy even though Joe knew Jimmy had become a part of Big Al Guglameno's new crew.

Big Al had spoken to Jimmy in secret, explaining that he wanted to put right all past ill-will between Aussie Joe and himself and wanted Jimmy to invite Joey for a friendly drink at the Terminus Hotel in Abbotsford. Just a friendly drink between young Jimmy and Aussie Joe – but don't mention that Al would show up a little later, as if by accident. Big Al explained that it would look better that way.

Young Jimmy Di Inzabella thought it was a good idea to smooth over any troubled waters between his new boss and his old mate so he rang Aussie Joe with a friendly and relaxed, casual invitation to join him for a few drinks and a get-together at the Terminus.

The pub had once been an underworld Collingwood bloodhouse but had since turned into a rather fashionable gathering place for writers, singers, actors and TV and film people, the arts and academic set.

Melbourne had buzzed with Chinese whispers – with a bit being added on each time the yarn was retold – about an eventual showdown between the Calabrian boss Guglameno and the Sicilian. The Sicilians had handed all day-to-day power, authority and control over Melbourne operations to the Calabrian clans, but, as long as Gravano stayed around to watch, Guglameno felt ill at ease. It all had to be sorted and young Jimmy felt he was doing his part in bringing the two men together. Even if it was a sort of sneaky way of doing it, he was sure it would be for the best.

Aussie Joe accepted the invitation from Jimmy and naturally thought the youngster had arranged this friendly drink on the orders of his grandfather, old Poppa Di Inzabella. Aussie Joe guessed the old man was about to move against Guglameno and was sending his grandson to sort out the details. At last, thought Joey, we can rid ourselves of this maggot once and for all. Joey thought for a moment to ring his uncle in Sicily, but decided against it. He couldn't keep waking the old man up with phone calls every time there was a new move on the chessboard.

Rome, September 1998. Sitting quietly on the sidewalk in front of the Cafe Trajon in a narrow laneway in the market area the Saietta family of brothers and cousins – Angelo, Bruno, Peppe, Aldo, Hugo, Mario, Carmine and Tito – were drinking red wine, eating plates of crab meat, lobster, anchovies, garlic and onions.

The waiter looked horrified, but dared not argue and went off to pour him a large glass of ice-cold Australian beer. Then Mario yelled out in Italian, 'Hey, waiter, eight beers please.'

The light luncheon was all very peaceful. They were sitting under an umbrella protecting them from the glare of the morning sun. It was a normal mid-morning Roman get-together and all was well. Italian criminals loved to mix up their food and wine. Years in prison did that to men, even if it horrified fine food and wine fanciers.

They lit up fat Dutch cigars and the sidewalk table erupted into clouds of blue smoke as the waiter carried out a long tray of beer in big glasses.

The diners drank a toast. 'God bless La Roma Societa Di Morte.' They were, of course, the ones who had extracted a million dollars ransom from Don Aspanu after kidnapping

Joey Gravano. They started talking business, about ripping off a tonne of high explosives from the Russians and selling it to the Arabs.

Then Hugo spoke up about something on his mind. 'I'm a bit puzzled by the lack of reaction from Poppa Aspanu. I thought revenge and a blood vendetta for sure.'

Angelo laughed. 'The Sicilians have lost it. If it wasn't for Hollywood, there would be no fucking mafia.'

As the group of men sat and chatted, a voluptuous whore walked past their table like a catwalk model, swinging a set of curvaceous hips and magnificent tits that bounced about like melons wrapped in a silk scarf. She was wearing a black clinging, wraparound dress and black Roman sandals.

About ten feet past the table where the Saietta family was seated, she stopped and bent over to inspect her left foot and gave a little whimper, as if she had caught a small stone in her sandal. Her massive bosoms almost fell out of her dress. All this display was aimed in the direction of the Saietta table.

'Holy mamma mia,' said Angelo Saietta. '*Lo zucchero, lo zucchero*.' Meaning sugar, sugar.

'Yeah,' said Bruno, 'she's got the biggest set of watermelons I've ever seen.'

'Hey,' yelled Peppe. '*Signorina, parla Italiano?*' Do you speak Italian? Not a real deep question, but it did the trick.

She looked up and flashed a wide smile and said, '*Si, Signore*.'

'My name is Peppe Saietta and these are my brothers and cousins, would you care to join us for a morning drink?' asked Peppe.

Would she ever. As she walked towards them, she said, 'My name is Carlotta.'

Tito yelled to the waiter, asked him his name, which was Carlo, and then said, 'OK, Carlo, bring Frizzante Bianco Vino (sparkling white wine) for this *panna montata madonna*.'

Carlotta blushed at being openly referred to as whipped cream – a Roman slang expression for what she was, a beautiful whore.

'Would you like something to eat, Carlotta?' asked Mario as he slipped a folded 100-dollar American note down her cleavage.

Carlotta smiled. 'Do you have any cetriolo with besciamella?'

They laughed appreciatively. Carlotta had just asked for cucumber with white sauce.

'My little one, for 100 American dollars how many cetriolo with besciamella can you eat?' asked Mario lewdly.

Carlotta looked around and counted the men quickly. '*Otto*,' she said, meaning eight. Then she smiled and put her left hand into Aldo's lap and squeezed him. Her right hand went into Mario's lap.

Mario cracked a joke and everybody laughed. It was just another good morning in Rome: eight gangsters and a whore all about to go off for a little harmless Italian romance before lunch …

None of them noticed the man in the long black overcoat about 15 feet away. It was Franco Di Tommaso. As he pulled the old wartime Beretta 9mm machine gun from under his coat, Carlotta the whore saw him and screamed out something about not having anything to do with the men at the table. She was too late. Repeated blasts from the 30-shot machine gun cut her screams short.

Carlotta and the eight Saiettas fell across the table, each other and the cobblestone laneway in a mish-mash of blood, wine and food. At such murderously close range a 9mm slug will pass through one body and into the next. But the killers were taking no chances. Luigi Monza stepped out from nowhere and sent a second spray of machine-gun fire. Monza smiled at Carlo the waiter and he and Di Tommaso walked away, got into a waiting Citroen car at the end of the laneway, and away they went.

'What was that girl trying to say?' asked Franco. 'It sounded like my name is Carlotta and I don't know these men,' replied Luigi.

'Poor slut,' said Di Tommaso. 'Wrong place, wrong time.'

'Lucky waiter,' said Luigi. 'He was two feet behind the girl and not a shot hit him.'

'Luck had nothing to do with it,' said Franco indignantly. 'We didn't come to fucking Rome to kill fucking waiters, you fucking stupido.'

'Sorry, Franco,' said Luigi. It was important to display manners at all times. It was just that the late Saietta family had put a hole in theirs by putting the snatch on Joey Gravano. Who, at that very moment, had a fresh problem rising up to meet him ...

The Terminus Hotel was a far cry from the way it had been. 'Jesus,' said Joey, 'they certainly have tarted this old joint up.'

Joey looked around the bar and shook his head. Young Jimmy Di Inzabella cleared his throat to attract Joey back to the land of here and now. 'Big Al Guglameno feels a bit sad about the bad blood between you and him, Joey,' he offered.

'Al Guglameno is a police informer, Jim,' grated Joe. 'You know it, and I know it.'

'No one can prove that, Joey,' said Jimmy, a little surprised that his olive branch looked like getting tossed on the floor.

'Yeah, well,' said Joey bitterly, 'if he's not a dog then he'll do till we get one. Ha ha.'

Jimmy laughed, too. 'Business is business, Joey,' he said.

'What?' replied Joey. 'So you approve?'

'No, no, no,' answered Jimmy. 'But times are changing. Sometimes we have to shake hands with the devil.'

Aussie Joe sneered at this. 'If ya lay down with dogs ya wake up with ya bottom getting sniffed, Jimmy,' he warned. 'What's this shit I hear about a gambling club Al opened. I thought the new Crown Casino, faggot mumbo-jumbo politicians and mummy's boy millionaires from south of the river fucked all the illegal gambling in Melbourne?'

Jimmy laughed and said knowingly, 'No video cameras in an illegal club, Joey.' Jimmy smiled and jumped in again with a message from his sponsor. 'The point is, Joey, the bad blood between the Sicilians and Calabrians is no good for any of us. Please, mate.'

'Who sent you?' asked Joey suddenly, and very seriously. 'I thought when you asked to see me that your old Padrino arranged it. What's all this talk of let's make friends with fucking Guglameno bullshit? Guglameno is a freaking big *noce di cocco*.' This meant 'coconut', but what it really meant was brown on the outside, white on the inside.

Jimmy was puzzled by Joey's use of the coconut reference. He knew that Scarchi Sicilians had a slang tongue all of their own but the expression was a new one on him. He looked at Joey and said in Italian, 'What?'

Joey smiled slyly. '*La noce di cocco*, Jimmy. The coconut is hard outside but soft inside. You see one colour on the outside, but the outside hides the inside?'

'I don't understand,' replied Jimmy in Italian.

Joey shot him an exasperated look, but explained himself patiently. 'Big Al is not what he pretends to be, Jimmy. Like all spies he shows one side and hides another – just like a coconut. Just remember when dealing with that false pretending dog, Jimmy, to look out. You understand?'

Jimmy nodded, thinking to himself Big Al was wrong if he thought there was any chance of making friends with this Sicilian hard head. Joey was old-time mafia in a young body. Such a man could not see the reason of business or compromise or negotiation. The Carlton attitude was to give a little to get a little, live and let live, all for the common good. For Joey there could be no shades of grey; it was either right or wrong, life or death, black or white.

Jimmy liked Joey but he knew Joey would never see reason. Joey asked for a light. As Jimmy held out a lit match, Joey noticed his hand was trembling slightly. Joey took his hand and looked into his friend's eyes and said in Italian softly,

'Why?' and Jimmy knew that Joey was starting to wonder just what this strange meeting was all about.

'OK,' said Joey, 'then what is this shit all about, Jimmy? Does this nonsense meeting have a point, and if it has then get to it, OK? And by the way, Jimmy, you don't speak fucking Italiano too good either. Who taught you to speak Italian – a fucking Frenchman with a hare lip?'

'I don't know,' said Jimmy. 'A bit from my mother, a bit from my father, I pick it up as I go.'

'Yeah, well, it's been nice, Jimmy. I don't know what the fuck this has been about but don't ring me again for another get-together drink unless ya got a reason. Sorry, *arrivederci*,' said Joey, 'and tell Al I'm not a fucking totally stupido, OK, Jimmy?'

Jimmy went pale.

'And get someone to teach you to talk Italian – it's fucking embarrassing trying to have a conversation with you,' said Joey as he got up to leave.

Jimmy looked at the clock again and wondered when Big Al would arrive. Wasn't he meant to bump into them by accident? Jimmy had a sick feeling that Big Al had involved him in some sort of set-up, but he still said to Joey, 'Don't go, mate. Hang around. What's the hurry?'

Joey looked at him hard. '*La mela cetriolo*, hey, Jimmy. *La mela cetriolo.*'

Jimmy froze. Joey had just said 'the apple cucumber'. Joey thought the whole thing was a set-up.

'No, no, Joey,' replied Jimmy.

'When?' asked Joey in Italian.

'No, no, Joey. I swear it's not. It's OK, I swear on my mother,' Jimmy implored.

Joey shot back: 'Your mother is dead, because this has got set-up written all over it. Why?' asked Joey.

Jimmy had tears in his eyes. 'Big Al asked me to talk to you,' he said.

Joey smiled. 'The devil always sends a trusted friend, Jimmy. I forgive you. It's not your fault. Ha ha, that Calabrian is smarter than I gave him credit.' And with that Joey walked out of the bar, sad but smiling.

Barry Mann and Hatter Hannigan, the mad cops, stood across the road from the pub. Hatter was softly singing a song he didn't know all the words to, so he invented his own.

Just then Aussie Joe Gravano stepped out of the pub door on to the footpath. Barry Mann nudged Hatter. 'Let's go,' he said.

As Joey walked towards his car, he sensed all was not well, but for some reason he wasn't gripped with any fear, just a quiet sense of fate. What will be will be. Maybe it was just his imagination. As he approached his car he caught sight of two men walking towards him and looked up to see Barry Mann and Hatter Hannigan.

'Hey, Gravano!' yelled Barry Mann.

Joey didn't need to ask who they were. He also knew as his right hand reached slowly under his coat for his .45 automatic that it was a futile gesture. But still he went for his gun. His brain screamed no and his heart screamed yes. Joey had been pushed too far.

'Don't do it, son!' yelled Hatter Hannigan as he reached for his revolver at the same time as Barry Mann reached for his. Then the two policemen stepped apart, giving Joey two targets.

As Joey raised his gun slowly he said to himself in Italian, 'I can't stop. Why?'

Joey's gun hand, his mind and his heart were all acting against each other. He saw the two men reach for their guns but he didn't take aim: he just fired blindly between them, closing his eyes as he did so like a mad zombie. Then he felt his chest and stomach explode and felt himself fall backwards. The cops had each punched three shots into Joey's chest and stomach and as he lay on the footpath he could hear the cries of fright from the crowd around him. He opened his eyes and saw Barry Mann looking down at him.

'Why did he go for his gun, Bazza?' asked Hatter.

Mann didn't reply. He just looked into the eyes of the dying Gravano.

'What's your name?' whispered Joey.

Mann replied, 'Barry Mann. Acting Detective Inspector Barry Mann, drug squad.'

Then Joey smiled, laughed and coughed blood.

'What's funny?' asked Hatter.

Then Joey replied as he died, 'I've been killed by the man who put the de bomp in the bomp de bomp. Ha ha.'

'What's he on about, Bazza?' asked Hatter.

'Private joke,' said the other detective.

As Joey's eyes closed, he heard Tina's voice calling him. He looked into the blackness to see a light and he heard her voice again. 'Joey, Joey, this way,' she called, and he followed the light. Then the words of the old rock and roll song came into his head.

'Who put the bomp in the bomp de bomp de bomp, who put the ring in the ding a ling a ding dong.' What a stupid thing for a man to think about as he died, thought Joey. Then the light came again and he could see Tina, still calling.

And Joey walked towards the light. It was at that moment that the crowd on the footpath saw him take his last breath. He was dead …

In Sicily, it was after midnight. Don Hector Aspanu woke in fright in his bed. He felt the chill of death on the hot Sicilian night.

'Joey,' called the Don, 'Joey, is that you?'

A knock came to the Don's door. It was Benny Benozzo, who was standing guard. 'You OK, Padrino?' called Benny.

Hector Aspanu felt the chill still and thought of Joey, but he called back to Benny, 'Fucking clams. I always dream when I eat clams.'

Don Hector still felt the chill then his left arm felt numb with pins and needles, and his heart felt like the devil was squeezing it. He called to Benny in Italian. 'I'm sick, Benny, call the doctor. Help, help.'

Then, silence.

The Don was dreaming. It was a long, complicated dream about him and his longlost love, Jayne Mansfield, back in the

1960s. He stirred. He could see a light above him and he rose up towards it and felt himself floating. Then he opened his eyes. He saw the faces of Bobby and Benny Benozzo and Franco Di Tommaso, Luigi Monza, young Carmine Baldassare and another man in a white coat, who looked like a doctor.

'Dottore?' asked the Don, and the doctor nodded and said, 'Si, Don Aspanu.'

'You save me, Dottore?' asked the Don.

'No,' said the doctor. 'Your men did. They got you to hospital in time.'

'Thank you,' said Hector to his men. 'Where is Joey?'

Luigi Monza spoke. 'We got a phone call from Melbourne an hour ago. Joey is dead.'

Don Hector nodded. 'I thought so, you know I felt him go. Where is Jayne Mansfield?'

The doctor spoke. 'Jayne Mansfield? Don Aspanu, she has been dead for a long time, many years now.'

'Ahh,' replied the Don, 'then it was all just a dream, a true dream, a sad dream but still just a dream. But, Joey, that was not a dream.'

'No,' answered Luigi. 'Joey is dead, I'm sorry, Don Hector.'

The Don nodded. 'I'm sorry also, Luigi. I'm sorry. And Jayne Mansfield isn't here?' he asked again.

His men shook their heads and looked at each other, puzzled by the old man's strange behaviour.

'Everyone is dead,' said the Don.

'But you are alive,' said the doctor, smiling.

'Not for long,' answered Don Hector. 'Not for long. Go now, all of you. Let me sleep and leave me to my dreams. Please go now. Get out, all of you.'

Sicily, 1973. Overlooking the waterfront of the fishing village of Catania stood the grand white marble villa of Catania's leading citizen, Don Pietro Baldassare, head of the Baldassare clan and a comrade in arms of Don Hector Aspanu.

Don Pietro was a man who had fathered many children to many women, but the apple of his eye was his youngest daughter, Clara. Unlike his other children, who all looked like something out of a Sicilian horror movie, Clara had her late mother's looks. In fact, she had been named after her dear-departed mother, Clara Massaria, the daughter of the old-time New York Moustache Pete mafia boss Giuseppe 'Joe the Boss' Massaria, who at one time controlled the biggest of the old-style mafia families in New York.

Don Pietro's love for his wife and his youngest daughter was the reason he named his grand villa La Casa Di Clara.

Young Clara Baldassare was 16 years old and quite extraordinary in the physical beauty department. Her silky, jet-black hair fell down to her waist. She had a deep-olive complexion but because her grandmother, Joe the Boss Massaria's wife, was from Northern Italy and had blonde hair and blue eyes, little Clara had inherited big green eyes. They gave her a mischievous look that fascinated any and every man who looked into them. Add the beautiful face to a teenage body that would tempt a priest, a set of hips and an arse that would arouse several regiments of the Greek Army and well-developed tits that made small Sicilian boys think of milk whenever she walked by.

Clara was a virgin, but passion burned inside her. She loved the attention she received from fishermen on the Catania waterfront and when her father went to Palermo on business she would don a specially imported black bikini from Paris, a little pair of black leather beach sandals and a black silk wraparound. From the outside she looked very respectable, until she undid the dress to reveal what was beneath.

Clara would wander down to the docks and make girlish chit chat with the Gamberetti and Gamberoni fishermen who fished the Strait of Messina separating Sicily from mainland Italy. The Gamberetti were shrimp fishermen; the Gamberoni fished for prawns. The fishermen were Clara's audience and she loved to play to them with a little teasing. She would swing herself about when she walked and was a source of sexual fascination for the fishermen and she knew it. While every man in the village knew her father and feared and respected him, and so treated her like the mother Mary, the fishermen had pirate blood and were a braver lot. They would call to Clara, 'Buon Giorno, Signoria Clara' or 'Buon Giorno, Signoria Baldassare.'

Some would yell, 'How are you, Clara?'

And she would stop and chat.

'What do you have for me today?' Clara would ask – meaning fish, shrimp and prawns – and they would invite her on to the boats to check the day's catch. It was on one of these invitations a year previously, at the tender age of 15, that Clara was introduced to a way of having all the men she wanted and still remain intact so she could come to her husband still technically a virgin on her wedding night. The result was that Clara had in a year sucked the dicks of nearly all the fishermen in the Port of Catania and, after what was at first a painful introduction to the Greek trick, as the fishermen called it, she had been regularly bashed in the buttocks by most of them. She was to the fishermen their little virgin putana – their virgin whore.

Every walk down to the wharf for Clara in the morning sunlight would not see her walk home again till the sun was setting. With the help of a goodly amount of strong Giallo grappa to drink, and fishermen to help her drink it, she would suck till her jaw ached. Then, using virgin olive oil as lubrication, they would take turns giving it to young Clara from behind.

Afterwards, Clara would lie in a hot soapy perfumed bath to get the smell of fish and fishermen off her. She knew that her conduct was dangerous, and that her sluttish activities on the waterfront were no secret, but she guessed that no one would dare repeat such foul gossip to her father. If they did, his blind rage could mean the death of every fisherman in Catania. If Clara was anyone else's daughter, she would be stoned in the streets or taken by the fishermen and sold to a brothel in Malta or Spain, Corsica or North Africa. But this angel-faced mafia Don's daughter would remain a Sicilian princess in spite of the fact she was a sick, twisted slave to sexual depravity.

And so it was that behind the back of the great and feared Don Pietro Baldassare his teenage daughter was known to the fishermen as the Bambino Pollo of Catania (the little chicken of Catania). They called her little chicken because she loved the cock so much. But, as the old Sicilian proverb goes, the grave is the only place to keep a secret in Sicily, so, when the outrageous rumour about Clara's outrageous behaviour reached the ears of Don Hector Aspanu, he had a problem indeed.

After all, little Clara was his god-daughter. She called him Uncle Hector, and wild yarns about her being shagged in the arse by every fisherman in the eastern ports of Sicily unsettled him, because it would be only a matter of time before his dear friend Pietro came to hear of it – and then what would happen? They would have to import fish from the mainland, for a start, because the Baldassare clan would kill every fisherman in Sicily.

Don Hector pondered the problem, but not for long. He knew that every Sicilian problem was solved with either a wedding or a funeral, and this was no different. Clara was not far off 17, and it was high time she was married, but it couldn't be to a man from Catania or even a native Sicilian as stories about the bride's love for the taste of cucumber and white sauce would soon reach the ears of her husband. And what of his dear friend Don Pietro? He wouldn't allow just anyone to have his pride and joy baby daughter. The only answer was to get baby Clara out of Sicily, properly married off to a wealthy Sicilian living in mainland Italy. Or even further away, thought Don Hector. Maybe France, Spain, America … or Australia.

Yes, thought the Don slyly, Australia was a nation of rat bags, hillbillies, Irish gunmen, English convicts, scoundrels and yuppie bum bandits. The Don thought of it as the last outpost, a desert fit for cowboys and psychopaths. And it was a long, long way from Sicily. So it was just the place for his knob-polishing, slackarsed little tart of a god-daughter. She could marry a wealthy Sicilian in Australia and drop dead, for all Don Hector cared. The main thing was the protection of the Baldassare family name. Maybe marriage and a funeral, he thought. Yes, that was it. Marry the whore off, then get her and her husband whacked. The Don was quite pleased with himself. If there was one thing he loved more than a good wedding, it was a good funeral, and with Clara Baldassare he could plan both.

Don Pietro Baldassare was surprised but secretly pleased when his dear and most trusted friend Don Hector Aspanu came to visit him with the offer for his daughter's hand in marriage from a young Sicilian businessman living in Australia. Not only was the young man in question a millionaire at the tender age of 27, he was a member of the clan. Aniello Massaria was his name – an Australian-born Sicilian and a recognised member of the Alderisio clan which was under the wing of the Aspanu clan and therefore the Baldassares.

Don Pietro listened in silence as Don Hector put the offer

to him and agreed to meet the young man in question. It would depend on Clara's yes or no. Don Pietro would not force his child into a loveless marriage, but Hector Aspanu was as good a matchmaker as he was a funeral director. He had selected Aniello Massaria with great care, taking into consideration the wishes of his friend Pietro for a good match, and the secret lusts of the prospective bride.

Aniello Massaria was a freak among sawn-off Sicilians, being well over six feet tall, handsome and strong as a young bull. He had inherited money from his family and had extensive interests in the Melbourne fishing and market garden industries. Through his interest in fishing, he imported heroin from the Philippines, and in his market gardens he grew massive crops of marijuana. He also had close links with the Calabrian Onorata Societa and the Naples Camorra. He lived by the code of silence, known by many and varied names. There is the one sure thing in the criminal world, be it in Italy or outer Mongolia: the rules change to suit the game daily. In the game Don Hector Aspanu was playing, he knew a wedding would unite two or three families – but that a funeral would bond them in blood forever. Providing, of course, he could place the blame for the deaths of Clara Baldassare and Aniello Massaria at the feet of others, he could direct revenge from the guns and knives of the Baldassare, Massaria and Alderisio clans towards an area of interest that would profit Don Hector Aspanu himself.

On the chessboard of the criminal world, to bring your

friends closer to you, you must give them an enemy you can both fight ... even if you have to create that enemy yourself.

Melbourne, 1974. It was a hot summer and young Joey Gravano was enjoying himself with his Thomastown-born Sicilian mates in the hotels and illegal brothels of Fitzroy Street and Grey Street, St Kilda.

It was an exciting time. The Melbourne sharpie wars had been raging since 1969, not to mention the painters and the dockers shootings. The dagos were losing every fight they tried on with the Aussie gangs, but among their ranks they were dominating the fledgling heroin market. They already controlled the marijuana market with the help of Aussie Bob Trimbole and his Calabrian hillbilly, dope-growing farmers. And they were gaining ground in the illegal gambling and prostitution rackets. But they couldn't win a round when it came to street battles and shoot-outs with the established Aussie criminal order. The Melbourne gunmen, toecutters, headhunters and standover men could just swoop in and take what they wanted, when they wanted.

Joey Gravano was one of the few Italians who saw that a war for control with the Aussie gangs was futile, and that the true power would be in taking silent control of the drug supply, rather than distribution. If the Italians and Chinese shared drug importing, the Aussies and the rest of the insane, blood-crazed rabble could kill each other for ever more in the endless wars fought over distribution.

Joey knew that in supply was real power. Why argue over a

glass of water with fools if you controlled the tap? Some Italians who couldn't see this insisted on getting into insane pissing competitions with mad men over street dealing. As far as Joey was concerned, they could all jump into their graves with his blessing. The Sicilians would remain friendly and smile at every one. 'Me no speak-a da English, me no want-a da trouble,' they'd say, and with the help of the Chinese they would quietly keep their hands on the tap. They had their ways of dealing with problems. An example of how they did was when Joey took the call from his uncle Hector in Sicily to attend to the little business of Aniello Massaria and his lovely young wife, Clara.

The whole conversation was Sicilian Scarchi code, which relied on fish names, animal names, the names of drinks, vegetables, fruits, meats and seafood, months of the year, days of the week, colours and numbers.

To someone in the know, one word could mean a whole sentence. The Sicilian tactic of killing a friend in secret then blaming it on an enemy in order to rally the clans in the name of the common good was known in Scarchi as the swordfish, or *La Pescespada*. If the body of the victim was never to be found it was *La Tonno*, the tuna. The Chinese triads were known as *La Riso*, the rice. A fire, or death by fire, was *La Pane Tostato*, the toast.

For the situation to remain as before, meaning that orders previously given should remain unchanged, then it was *La Menu a prezzo fisso* – the set menu. A coward was *La Coniglio* (the rabbit) and a person to be killed was *La Anatra* (the duck). If a bribe was needed they spoke of butter. If a friend was a bit mad and was to be watched he was noodles. Sunday was the day of death. A bad idea was black, and a good one was white. If you had the answer to a problem and could solve it, you had the key. If you were given the Don's nod to proceed, you were given a stamp. To be sent a newspaper was to be sent coded written instructions. In old Sicily, Jews had to paint their houses blue, so a Jew was *La Azzurro*; a double killing was a postcard. To give someone soap was to kid them along with smiles and nice lies before they were killed. The only time Interpol broke the Sicilian Scarchi code was when they kept talking over the phone about marijuana and naturally referred to it as *La Verde* (the green) so they changed it to *La Cavolo* (the cabbage).

This time, Hector Aspanu wanted Joey to do the Swordfish. Joey knew that the politics behind the order was none of his business. He knew only that obeying orders would elevate him overnight in the ranks of his clan. So, if the old man back in Sicily wanted the Swordfish, the Swordfish it would be.

Aniello and Clara Massaria lived on a farm in far western Victoria. They had 1500 acres with 200 of them on the South Australian side of the state border. For Clara, it was a long way from Sicily, but Aniello was built like a Greek God, with the face of a Roman prince and the dick of a Welsh pony. As was his right as a Sicilian husband, he gave Clara a good beating with his belt on the night of their wedding in Catania. This was because she made the mistake of questioning him when he ordered her to hand over the wedding purse so he could count the cash.

'That's my money,' said Clara.

She was beaten till she screamed for mercy, then Aniello pulled out his wedding gift and took her virginity with a violence that made her scream in pain. Aniello was delighted to find the sheets red with virgin blood.

However, when Aniello got his young bride back to Australia and, having drunk a little too much one night, forgot his manners and ordered her to go down, he began to suspect he'd been sold a used car. One that had copped a few bananas in the diff, at that. He suspected this because Clara, having also partaken of a little too much vino, forgot to say, 'Oh no, my husband, you'll have to show me how.' Instead, she promptly proceeded to give him the hottest, deep-throat blow-job he had ever had in his life. This resulted in the jealous Sicilian accusing her of being an experienced vacuumer in the fly department and, after another savage beating, she confessed and told all. With the result that he beat her near to death and made her sleep in the chicken shed, chained to the wall like a howling dog.

Aniello Massaria was insane with rage. That old Sicilian pirate Aspanu had sold him some little whore who had swallowed more swords than a circus performer. Naturally Aniello would have to kill her, but it must look like an accident, or suicide, lest her father and old Aspanu kill him. Aniello thought furiously how this Sicilian marriage had been pushed on him with far too many smiles, and now he knew why. Now all Sicily was having a good laugh at him. Soon, thought Aniello, when the whore with the arse like a Greek bucket returns to Sicily in a coffin, the laughter would turn to tears …

All of which explains why, when Joey Gravano made the long night drive over to the property, he got there just in time to receive the sad news of the death of young Clara Massaria. The result, it was said, of a tragic accident while she was trying to climb through a barbed-wire fence, carrying a loaded shotgun.

As Joey drove along in the hope of finding some small country town with a phone box that worked, the local news on the car radio informed him that a market gardener, Mr Aniello Massaria, had been arrested by Victoria police for the murder of his wife, Clara. By the time Joey found a phone box, both the Victorian and South Australian police had located a marijuana crop on the Massaria farm valued at two million dollars and were arguing over who should make the arrest. It seemed that, while Mrs Massaria was shot on the South Australian side of the property, the marijuana crop had 50 acres either side of the border.

When Joey rang Sicily and informed his uncle of this interesting turn of events, he was told to forget it and get out of there. Massaria had spilled his guts to police in return for a manslaughter charge instead of a murder blue, and police were arresting Italians in both states.

Within 24 hours, there were calls for a Royal Commission into mafia involvement in the marijuana industry. Aussie

Bob Trimbole's name was mentioned along with about anyone whose name ended in a vowel. Suddenly the newspapers were screaming about an honoured society. Every dago dirt farmer who grew a little dope between his tomatoes had suddenly become part of the mafia. So much for the code of silence.

When he rang Joey a week after the news, the Don didn't know whether to laugh or cry. 'Well, Joey,' he said, 'Pietro's baby Clara is a virgin again. Death can do that even to a whore – but this swordfish has just stabbed us all in the arse.'

'So what do we do now?' asked Joey.

'Simple,' said the Don. 'Tell the boys to start growing their dope in New South Wales. Ha ha.'

Sicily, 1998. Don Hector Aspanu had just told his men the story of Clara and Aniello Massaria, and how Massaria had vanished to Canada after doing a secret deal with a Royal Commission.

The old man hung his head and shook it as if, even in retelling the story, he still couldn't believe it.

'So we never got him?' asked Bobby Benozzo, surprised.

'No,' answered the Don. 'We think he opened a pizzeria in Canada and got involved with the De Carlo family. We send some boys over and shot the wrong man. The pizzas stunk too. The whole thing was a fucking nightmare.'

The group was sitting in the shade under the giant lemon tree in the courtyard of the Don's villa in Montelepre. He was very old and wanted only to sit and drink grappa. The bodyguards sat with him, and around the courtyard stood a handful of silent, hard-faced Sicilian gypsies carrying loaded rifles. Palermo was in uproar as the Delle Torre clan and Baldassare clan had gone to war with each other over control of the Aspanu clan.

Don Hector had ordered that his favourite grandson, Little Hector, be taken to safety in the hills with his gypsy friends.

The Don had ordered the death of his remaining sons and grandsons, using the squabble between the Delle Torre and Baldassare clans over the family empire as a smother to kill off Aspanu family members he considered surplus to requirements. He knew they would never be able to run the clan properly. They were spoiled, greedy yuppies and he was ashamed of them. That is why the old Don had loved Joey so much. Joey was the only one who could have run the family.

'You know who I blame for the downfall of La Mafia?' he asked suddenly.

'No,' said Franco. 'Who?'

The men smiled, sensing one of the Don's jokes.

'Mario fucking Puzo and Giorgio fucking Armani, that's who. Between the two of them every Italian criminal in the world is now more interested in what they fucking wear than who they kill, and real-life mafia guys are now trying to imitate Hollywood. The whole thing is too much for me.'

One of the stony-faced gypsies walked up and whispered in the Don's ear. The old man nodded and laughed. He raised his glass and said, '*E nomine patre et file espiritus santos*. My sons are all dead.'

The men looked at each other. The old man sitting with them in the shade drinking grappa and making comedy about seagulls and pushbikes, Mario Puzo and Giorgio Armani was one of the few mafia dons left on earth who could order the death of his own children so control of his clan not fall into their hands. This was the action of a Caesar. Were they witnessing the death of the last true Sicilian? All Don Hector's men knew that when the Don died they would either all die with him if they didn't attack in the name of the Don's hand-picked grandson and continue to defend the Aspanu clan until the boy came of age to take control. The men were determined to march forward carrying the corpse of the old Don on their shoulders.

'So,' said the Don thickly, 'what do we know about the cocksuckers who shot Joey?'

Luigi Monza replied to this question. 'It was the two Victorian policemen, Padrino. Drug squad. A couple of mad Irish. A detective called Herbert Hannigan and his boss, an Inspector Barry Mann.'

'Who did you say?' asked the Don.

'Hannigan,' replied Monza.

'No, no, the other one' asked the Don.

'Mann,' replied Monza. 'Barry Mann.'

The Don started to laugh. 'What's funny?' asked Franco.

'Bomp de bomp,' laughed the Don. 'Poor Joey got killed by the man who put the bomp in the bomp de bomp de bomp. Ha ha.'

The men looked at each other, puzzled by this mumbo

jumbo, but not wanting to say so. They hadn't spent time in America like him.

'The old song,' said the Don, but still the men didn't get the comedy. 'Ahh, forget it,' snarled the Don. He was caught in a cultural wasteland. 'More grappa.' His glass was promptly filled.

As he reached for his glass his hand shook, he gave a faint groan and his hand fell limply to his side.

The gypsies stood in silence and the men sitting with the Don looked at each other, then at the old man, too frightened to speak.

Monza spoke first. 'Padrino, Padrino,' he said, but the old man didn't hear the call.

'Don Hector,' said Franco, but the Don didn't reply.

The Benozzo brothers had tears in their eyes. Monza reached out to touch his Don.

Franco said, 'Don't wake him.'

Benny Benozzo said sadly. 'No, Franco, no one can wake him now. La Padrino is no more. *La morte, la morte.*'

The bell of the Montelepre church rang out and in reply men fired guns into the air. Don Hector Aspanu was dead but not forgotten. His clan and the mafia army he had controlled for half a century rose up and, as the coffin was carried through the streets of Montelepre, gunmen were sent to all parts of Sicily to kill the last of the old man's enemies. Don Aspanu would not die alone.

As Franco Di Tommaso, Luigi Monza and Benny and Bobby Benozzo stood by the grave of their Padrino surrounded by

700 men of the 14 separate families that made up the clan Aspanu, Monza asked Di Tommaso, 'What now, Franco, what now?'

Di Tommaso replied, 'The Don once told me when we were talking about Joey and his silly chess games that a war may take a hundred years to fight, and in that hundred years there can be a thousand battles. And for every battle we win we might lose two. But for every man we lose we take two of theirs, for every man who dies leaves a son, a grandson, a nephew, a brother, an uncle or a friend who will pick up the dead man's weapon.

'We win today, lose tomorrow. The point is, win or lose, we are the one enemy that simply will not go away. They can defeat us for a hundred years, but if we don't go away then we win. Kill one generation and the next takes its place.

'You see, an enemy who will never surrender is an enemy who will never be defeated. And, as the Don said, in the end that is the Sicilian Defence.'

Now you can buy any of these other *Chopper* books by
Mark Brandon Read from your bookshop or direct from
his publisher.

Free P+P and UK Delivery
(Abroad £3.00 per book)

Chopper
ISBN 978-1-84454-349-6 PB   £6.99

Chopper 2 – How to Shoot Friends and Influence People
ISBN 978-1-84454-382-3 PB   £6.99

Chopper 3 – Hell Hath No Fury Like a Mate Shot in the Arse
ISBN 978-1-84454-040-2 PB   £6.99

Chopper 4 – Happiness is a Warm Gun
ISBN 978-1-84454-094-5 PB   £7.99

Chopper 5 – Don't Go Breaking My Legs
ISBN 978-1-84454-269-7 PB   £7.99

Chopper 6 – A Bullet in Time Saves Nine
ISBN 978-1-84454-502-5 PB   £7.99

Chopper 7 – Gentlemen Prefer Guns
ISBN 978-1-84454-355-7 PB   £7.99

Chopper 8 – A Bullet in the Head is Worth Two in the Chamber
ISBN 978-1-84454-535-3 HB   £17.99
ISBN 978-1-84454-769-0 PB   £7.99

Chopper 10 – A Fool and his Toes are Soon Parted
ISBN 978-1-84454-741-8 HB   £17.99

TO ORDER SIMPLY CALL THIS NUMBER
+ 44 (0) 207 381 0666

Or visit our website www.johnblakepublishing.co.uk

Prices and availability subject to change without notice